This book was published to accompany the Exhibit "The Rediscovered Face – The Unmistakable Features of Christ" organized for the 34th edition of the Meeting for Friendship among Peoples

The Exhibit "The Face of Jesus: From that Gaze, the Human Person Is Born" was organized in the United States with the help of:

First English Edition, December 2013

© 2013 Human Adventure Books, Tampa (Florida)
ISBN 978-0-9823561-8-0

First Italian Edition, July 2013

© 2013 Edizioni di Pagina, Bari (Italy)

Curators
Emanuele Colombo, Michele Colombo, Paolo Martinelli OFM Cap, Paola Francesca Moretti, Giovanna Parravicini, Maria Cristina Terzaghi, Raffaella Zardoni

With help from
Paul Badde, Gregory M. Pell, Arianna Petraccia, Heinrich W. Pfeiffer S.J., Davide Rondoni, Marco Rossi, Silvana Tassetto, Paola Vismara

With the generous support of
The Franciscan Institute of Spirituality Pontifical University Antonianum; The Order of Friars Minor; Province of Pescara; Faith and Culture in Abruzzo; The Way of St Thomas the Apostle.

The exhibit organizers are grateful to the following people for allowing access to archives, documentation, and audiovisual material
The Capuchin Friars of the Convent in Manoppello, Paul Badde, Antonio Bini

Every effort has been made to obtain permission to reproduce the images in this volume. If any of the images have not been released with due permission, please contact the publisher.

The Rediscovered Face
The Unmistakable Features of Christ

written by
Emanuele Colombo, Michele Colombo,
Paola Francesca Moretti, Giovanna Parravicini,
Silvana Tassetto, Maria Cristina Terzaghi,
Raffaella Zardoni

translated by
Raymond Frost, Amanda Murphy, Chris Vath

TABLE OF CONTENTS

Foreword – The Face of Christ — 7
Cardinal Seán O'Malley

Introduction – The *Acheiropoieton* Images of Christ
— 9

"We Would Like to See Jesus"
The *Kamouliana* and the *Mandylion* — 12

The *Kamouliana* — 12
The Iconoclastic Controversy p. 13

The *Mandylion* from Edessa — 14
Abgarus' Letter p. 14

The Sack of Constantinople — 18
- Icon and Relic *Giovanna Parravicini* — 20

"Is This Then What Thy Face Was Like?"
The Roman Veronica — 22

The First Indulgence — 23
- "He Is Indulgent with Us" *Davide Rondoni* — 28

Veronica, the Bleeding Woman — 30

The Holy Years — 33

What Was the Veronica Like? — 42
Dark and Luminous p. 42 • Bloodied and Crowned with Thorns p. 48

- The Cult of the Veronica in Illuminated Manuscripts
  Silvana Tassetto — 50
- The *Opusculum de sacrosancto Veronicae sudario*
  Paola F. Moretti — 54

"Men Have Lost a Face"
The Modern Era — 56

The Sack of Rome 1527 — 57
A New Veronica? — 60
The Holy Face between 1800 and 1900 — 63

"An Eternal Imprint"
The Veil of Manoppello — 67

The Arrival of the Veil — 68
- The Historical Authenticity of the *Relatione*: Verifications and New Data *Arianna Petraccia and M. Cristina Terzaghi* — 71
- The Copies of the Historical Account *Michele Colombo* — 72

The Unmistakable Features of Christ — 73
Superimposition with the Face of the Shroud p. 75 • The *Kamouliana* p. 76 • The *Mandylion* and the *Keramion* p. 77 • The Transparency of the Veil p. 78 • The Visible Teeth p. 79 • Signs of Suffering p. 82

Final Questions — 82

"Whoever Contemplates Me, Consoles Me" — 85

Donato da Bomba — 85
Karol Wojtyła — 89
Luigi Giussani — 89
Paolo Martinelli — 90
Angelo Scola — 91
Bruno Forte — 93
Benedict XVI — 96

Appendix – Veronica Route — 100
Notes on the Veronica Route website — 101

References — 102
Notes — 107

FOREWORD
THE FACE OF CHRIST

For us as Catholics, there is a long and sacred history of venerating the holy images of our Lord, Jesus Christ. At Christmas time, we incense the Holy Infant in the manger and recall his humility and love. During Lent we walk with devotion through the Stations of the Cross, tracing the steps that lead to our salvation. And on Easter morning we stand before the empty tomb, filled with awe in the presence of the Angels at the wondrous works that God has done. Images of Christ have the power to move our hearts, they can catechize without words and allow us to contemplate the beautiful face of God revealed in His own Son.

Images of Christ are also signs for the Church on pilgrimage. As pilgrims we know that we walk through this world with our eyes "fixed on Jesus" so that He may be for us "the Way, the Truth, and the Life." Throughout the centuries, Jesus' face has been depicted in a number of different ways. At times He is depicted as the one who suffers in His Passion, out of love for humanity. At other times He is shown as the one who teaches and who invites disciples to follow Him. And still there are other depictions of Christ in Glory, bearing the wounds of his passion as a sign of his love and proof of his sacrifice for us. These images are all meant to accompany us in life and give us hope and strength.

When we were children, they used to read us the story about a king who was a good man. He decided he would disguise himself as a peasant so that he could go and live amongst his subjects. He wanted to experience their sufferings and know their aspirations. As moving as this story might be, the Incarnation of the Son of God is quite different. In the Incarnation, Jesus does not come disguised as one of us but He comes as one of us, a brother. He does not come to get to know us. He comes so we can get to know Him, our God. He is the revelation. He is the event. He has not come for a short visit but to insert Himself into our history permanently. He is with us. He is our contemporary.

Fr Giussani's charism has helped so many young people discover Christ in their lives. It is in the Church, in communion, that we have the best opportunity to experience Christ and His friendship. The poison of our contemporary culture is the extreme individualism of the age, which is documented in Professor Putnam's study on Americans, *Bowling Alone*,[1] in which Putnam demonstrates how each generation of Americans is becoming more and more isolated, more and more alienated. There are more people living alone, eating alone, and spending hours before a television or computer screen alone. In His Incarnation, God is with us and will never abandon us. He comes to take us out of our isolation and invites us into true friendship and communion.

As we look upon the face of Christ in this exhibit, I invite you to meditate on those words

He spoke to St Peter: "Who do you say that I am?" He wants us to know Him and to know how much He loves us. He wants us to be leaven in our world, a light that will help others discover God's presence, His Love and His Beauty so that you and I can share that with the whole community. I pray that this exhibit of the face of Christ will draw those who look upon it to discover in it the face of love and mercy, the face of the one who calls us to follow Him.

Cardinal Seán O'Malley, OFM Cap.

Fig. 1 (*facing*). *Christ Leaves His Face Imprinted on a Cloth to Fulfil King Abgarus' Wish*, MS Lat. 2688, Jesus' Infancy Gospel and Stories of the Image of Edessa, 1280-1285, f. 75; Paris, Bibliothèque Nationale.

INTRODUCTION
THE *ACHEIROPOIETON* IMAGES OF CHRIST (NOT MADE BY HUMAN HANDS)

At the dawn of Christianity, the rapidly spreading Christian communities abided by the biblical prohibition against making images[2] of God, which was sustained by authoritative voices such as that of Eusebius from Caesarea.[3] The prohibition was backed up by an understandably prudent attitude among Christians, who hesitated to represent the figure of Christ directly, due to the anti-Christian persecutions of the first centuries after Christ. These persecu-

Fig. 2. Rembrandt, *If People Do These Things When the Tree Is Green*, 1655-1660, pen and ink, detail; Haarlem, Teylers Museum.

Fig. 3. *The Holy Face*, Manoppello (Pescara), Shrine of the Holy Face.

tions only ended with the Edict of Tolerance, promulgated in Milan by Constantine in 313 A.D.

The first representations of Christ are therefore either symbolic, i.e. comprehensible to very few, or they hark back to classical models, such as the philosopher with a bushy beard, the beardless young god Apollo or the good shepherd, represented as a young man.

It is only from the fifth to the sixth century that in both East and West the face in which we all recognize the features of Christ begins to become prevalent. Nothing similar happened for the Virgin Mary, whose portraits do not necessarily have features in common.

Many reasons have been put forward for this doctrinal and iconographic change. For the Fathers of the Church, its origin lies in the Church's awareness that it possessed a portrait of Christ of miraculous origins. A monk, George of Cyprus, was witness to this during the iconoclastic controversy, when he wrote that "Christ Himself transmitted His image to the Church."[4]

The existence of an *acheiropoieton* image (not made by human hands) is recorded in two significant accounts. In the East, we read of the *Mandylion*, a cloth on which Jesus apparently left an imprint of His face, in response to a request from King Abgarus of Edessa [fig. 1], and in the West, we read of the veil which Veronica was said to have used to wipe Christ's face on the way to Calvary.

Literary and historical sources record a still more ancient portrait on cloth, named *Kamouliana* after the small town in Cappadocia where it was found. Taken to Constantinople in 574, the image was to accompany the Emperor during his campaigns in Africa and Persia as the imperial banner.

On September 1, 2006, Pope Benedict XVI visited a small sanctuary on the slopes of the Majella mountain, where the Holy Face of Manoppello is kept. This is a portrait of Christ on a semi-transparent veil which cannot be attributed to any technique of painting on canvas or cloth [fig. 3]. These four images are the *acheiropoieta* discussed in the present account. They are all on cloth and only depict the still living face of Christ.

Another characteristic shared by the four veils a lack of clarity surrounding the appearance and disappearance of each portrait, rendering their historical reconstruction complex and controversial, despite a period of fame that certifies their existence. Three of these veils are considered lost. The *Kamouliana* disappeared at an unknown time before the iconoclastic controversies, as did the *Mandylion* during the sack of Constantinople in 1204. The fame of the Roman "Veronica" began to dwindle following the sack of Rome in 1527 (even though a faded image is still kept in St Peter's). The veil of Manoppello is the only one which remains to us. According to a parchment dated 1646, it arrived in the town after which it was named at the turn of the sixteenth century.

The aim of this itinerary is to get to know the stories of these portraits and reflect on what the gift that Christ Himself left has meant, and could mean, for us.

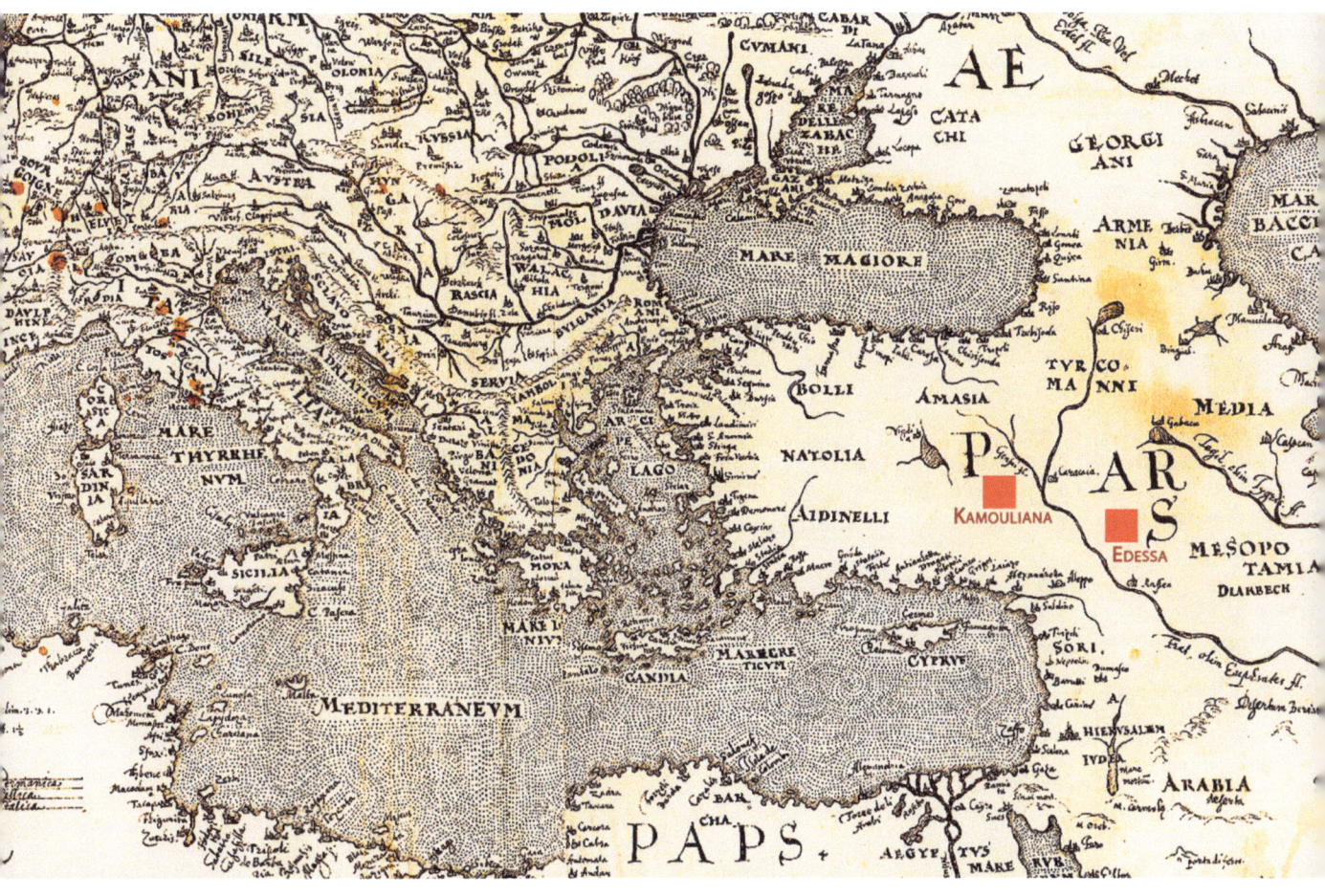

"WE WOULD LIKE TO SEE JESUS"
THE *KAMOULIANA* AND THE *MANDYLION*

Now there were some Greeks among those who had come up to worship at the feast. They came to Philip, who was from Bethsaida in Galilee, and asked him, "Sir, we would like to see Jesus." [Jn 12:20-21]

The *Kamouliana*

It is in the small town of Kamouliana, in Cappadocia, in present-day Turkey, that the story of an image of Christ begins – an image on cloth, not made by human hands. A sermon attributed to St Gregory of Nyssa calls the town of Kamouliana 'New Bethlehem'.[5] The image thus creates a strong tie with the mystery of the Incarnation. The existence of the image in the Byzantine world has been attested to since the times of Justinian (482-565) in liturgical and historical sources which allow us to follow its progress up to the beginning of the eighth century. There is, however, no reproduction[6] of the *Kamouliana* [fig. 4].

The sources do not agree on the details of the appearance of the *Kamouliana*. The oldest testimony, attributed to Zachariah from Mitilenus, at the end of the fifth century, recounts that a pagan woman named Hypatia, who could not believe in Christ unless she saw him, found the cloth floating in her well. This is in line with the theme, attributed to the Greeks, of the need to see in order to believe. It is said that other copies were miraculously made of this original image. The *Kamouliana*, or a copy of it, reached Diobulone, in Pontus, and from there was carried in procession throughout Asia Minor for two years.[7]

In 574 Justinus II had the *Kamouliana* taken to Constantinople where it was triumphantly

Fig. 4 (*facing*). *Icon of Saints Sergius and Bacchus*, 6th-7th century, encaustic; Kiev, Bogdan and Varvara Khanenko Museum of Arts (from the Monastery of St Catherine of Sinai). The image of Christ inside the clypeus could be a rare reproduction of the *Kamouliana*.

Fig. 5 (*below*). *Iconoclasm and Scenes from Christ's Passion*, MS D 129, Chludov Psalter, c. 850-875 f. 67, detail; Moscow, State Historical Museum.

acclaimed as the imperial banner, the dispenser of divine protection over the city and the empire.[8] Before the victory on the river Arzamon, Theophylactus Simocattus describes the *Kamouliana*, "the image of God incarnate"[9], as an image which seems to be neither woven nor painted:

"[...] it has been said since ancient times and to the present day that divine art created it, that it was not produced either by a weaver's hands nor was it painted by the colors of a painter."[10]

In 622, George of Pisidia wrote that Heraclius, departing for Persia, "took the divine and venerated figure, the copy of the writ that was not written by human hands."[11]

News of the *Kamouliana* ceased suddenly, just before the iconoclastic controversy (726-843). We do not know when or how the image was lost or forgotten. During the Second Nicean Council (787), in which the legitimacy of icons was discussed, the *Kamouliana* is cited just once as a thing of the past, when the deacon Cosmas showed a martyrology from which the pages on the story of the *Kamouliana* had been torn, to show how the iconoclasts had wanted to destroy the testimonies of the Eastern Fathers in favor of icons.[12]

The Iconoclastic Controversy

In the war against sacred images (the meaning of the term "iconoclasty"), which tore the Byzantine Empire and the Eastern Church apart for more than a century, the conflict was first and foremost theological, and concerned the mystery of Christ. Those who opposed the making of images maintained that to depict Christ meant to depict only human nature (since divine nature cannot be circumscribed), which therefore divided the unity of His Person.

The reach of iconoclastic ideology went beyond the limits of the heresy which was fought against in the eighth and ninth centuries and re-appeared among Protestants, albeit with significant differences. Paradoxically, it was not born from the negation of Christianity, but from the ever-present temptation of false spiritualism, which declared boundless respect for the divinity to the bitter end, to the point of refusing contamination by any material representation. This position proposes a dualism, which ends up by doubting the reality of the Incarnation itself. As Solov'ev observed,

"to claim that divinity cannot be sensibly expressed or externally manifested, or that the divine power cannot employ visible and symbolic

means of action, is to rob the divine incarnation of all its reality."[13]

The defenders of images, called the iconodules, asked their opposition, "How will you recognize Christ on His return if you lose the memory of His personal face?"[14]

The *Mandylion* from Edessa

Although the Fathers of the Council forgot the *Kamouliana*, during the discussions at the Council another *acheiropoieton* image was mentioned several times, as an argument in favor of icons. This was the *Mandylion* from Edessa, which was a towel (*mandylion* means 'towel' or 'handkerchief' in Arabic) that the Lord Himself allegedly sent to King Abgar the Black (4 B.C.- 50 A.D.). It was to become the most famous image of the Byzantine world:

"It is said that King Abgarus of Edessa had sent a painter to make a portrait of Christ. But he was not able to do it because of the light that shone out of the Lord's Face. So, taking a veil and placing it before his holy and life-giving face, Jesus impressed his image on it and sent it to King Abgarus, thus satisfying his desire."[15]

Thus St John of Damascus sums up the story of Abgarus V, toparch of Edessa (present-day Urfa in Turkey) who was a contemporary of Christ's. According to tradition, Abgarus introduced Christianity into his kingdom, after hearing the preaching of Taddeus, one of the seventy disciples, who had been sent to Edessa by the apostle Thomas. Even today the churches of Syrian origin venerate King Abgarus as a saint.

There is a great deal of historical and liturgical documentation about the *Mandylion*. The most ancient documents date back to the fourth century. In those of Syrian origin, the ambassadors of King Abgarus are identified with the Greeks who approach Philip, saying "We would like to see Jesus", quoted in Chapter XII of the Gospel of St John.

Abgarus' Letter

The story of King Abgarus [fig. 6] is told by Symeon the Metaphrast in the liturgical lectionary called the Synaxarion.[16] Towards the year 30, Abgarus V, the governor of Edessa, could find no doctor nor medicine which could cure him of his leprosy and gout. Having heard about the miracles Jesus was working in Jerusalem in the midst of the ingratitude of the Jews, he summoned Ananias, his secretary, who was an excellent portrait painter. Ananias was to carry out two tasks: hand a letter to Jesus and then paint his portrait, as true to life as possible. The text of the letter reads thus:

"Abgarus Uchama the toparch to Jesus the good Saviour that hath appeared in the parts (place) of Jerusalem, greeting. I have heard concerning thee and thy cures, that they are done of thee without drugs or herbs: for, as the report goes, thou makest blind men to see again, lame to walk, and cleansest lepers, and castest out unclean spirits and devils, and those that are afflicted with long sickness thou healest, and raisest the dead. And having heard all this of thee, I had determined one of two things, either that thou art God come down from heaven, and so doest these things or art a Son of God that doest

Fig. 6. *King Abgarus' Stories*, MS 382, Menology, 1063, f. 192v, detail; Moscow, State Historical Museum. This iconography is inspired by the Sinai triptych.

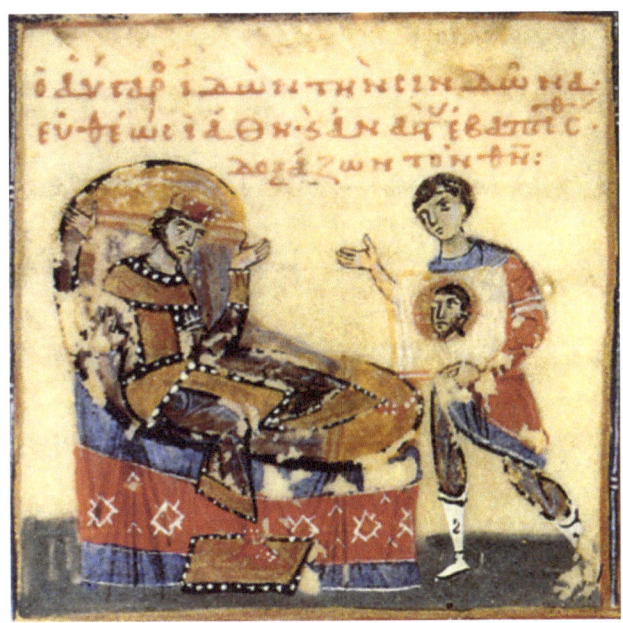

these things. Therefore now have I written and entreated thee to trouble thyself to come to me and heal the affliction which I have. For indeed I have heard that the Jews even murmur against thee and wish to do thee hurt. And I have a very little city but comely, which is sufficient for us both."[17]

Ananias went to Jerusalem, delivered the letter and tried to paint the portrait requested, but he did not succeed because "the face of Christ shone with such intense light that it could not be painted." Understanding Ananias' difficulty, Jesus asked for some water and a towel, and imprinted the image of His face on the towel which He then handed to Ananias, together with a written answer to King Abgarus, in which He promised to send Abgarus His disciple Taddeus. Abgarus treated the letter and the portrait with great honor and deep veneration, and was healed of his ills by the portrait, except for a few spots of leprosy left on his face.

The correspondence between Abgarus and Jesus was well known in ancient times. The historian Eusebius claimed to have translated it from Syrian into Greek. Egeria, a pilgrim to Edessa in 384, asked the bishop for a copy to compare with the version she had seen in Spain. Augustine knew of the correspondence but disputed its authenticity. Neither Eusebius nor Egeria mention the portrait of Christ, which can be found in versions of the account dated around the mid-fourth century.

Having received the portrait, Abgarus placed it in a niche at the gates of the city. When the city returned to paganism, the bishop of the city sealed the niche with a tile so as to protect the image. It was four centuries before the

Fig. 7. The Bishop discovers the *Mandylion* image imprinted on the tile (*Keramion*): the lamp is still burning, 14th century; *Mandylion* of Genoa, Church of St Bartholomew of the Armenians, detail of the gilt silver frame.

Fig. 8 (facing). *Arrival of the Mandylion in Constantinople*, Madrid Skylitzes, MS Vitr. 26-2, Synopsis of the Story, 13th century, f. 131; Madrid, Libreria Nacional de España.

image was rediscovered, during the siege by King Khosrau of Persia. The lamp that had been placed inside the niche was still burning and the flame had helped create a copy of the image on the stone covering it [fig. 7]. This copy took the name of *Keramion*, "tile", or "ceramic" in Greek.

The first reliable historical source which mentions an image not made by human hands kept in Edessa is dated 590;[18] Arab sources also mention the cloth on which Jesus imprinted the image of His face.

At the end of the iconoclastic controversy, when the cult of images was permitted once again, the *Mandylion* continued to interest Byzantium, which desired to possess the image of Christ, partly to remove it from the Muslim-dominated city of Edessa. In 944, after a large ransom had been paid, the most venerated image of the East arrived in Constantinople [fig. 8], amidst wondrous events, healings and great rejoicing among the people, and was welcomed by Emperor Romanus I, the Lecapenus (920-944).[19]

In Constantinople, the question of when the image was formed was immediately posed, showing that the link with King Abgarus was not considered certain. According to Emperor Constantine VII (944-959), the image could have been made either according to Abgarus' account, and therefore during Jesus' public life, or during the agony in the Garden of Olives:

"On the main points, everyone agrees that the image was imprinted in wondrous fashion on the cloth by our living Lord's face. But there is disagreement about the moment when this happened, which does not harm the truth in any way, regardless of when the image was formed. Here is the account of the other tradition: 'When Christ was about to submit voluntarily to his passion, when he showed his human weakness and was seen in agony, while praying, when his sweat ran like drops of blood, according to the Gospel, then, it is said, he was given a piece of cloth by one of his disciples, which can still be seen now, and he dried his sweat. Immediately, this visible imprint of his living features appeared on the cloth.'"[20]

From this text, it can be deduced that the *Mandylion* bore evidence of Jesus while He was still alive, but suffering.

From the tenth century on, the theological reflections in defense of icons together with the great importance attributed to the mystery of the Incarnation brought about a minor artistic and liturgical revolution. As new churches sprang up, the *Mandylion* and the *Keramion* were placed at the apex of arches facing east and west [fig. 9], and each other, where they touched the heavens (in the cupola) and the earth (the cube of the nave) [fig. 13].

Reproductions of the *Mandylion* can also be found on top of *tympana* on church exteriors and on the gates of cities. Moreover, because of its unique nature as a portrait left to us by Christ Himself, the Holy Face became the prototype of all icons of Christ.[21] As Olivier Clément wrote:

"Indeed, something was truly discovered in sixth century Edessa, and carried triumphantly to Constantinople in 944, something which

Fig. 9. *Mandylion*, 11th century, presbytery fresco; Cappadocia (Turkey), Göreme, Sakli Kilise.

gave precise details about the features of Christ."²²

Quite uniquely, August 16 is a feast day in the Eastern calendar dedicated to the arrival of the *Mandylion* in Constantinople. At first, the *Mandylion* was available in Constantinople to be venerated and copied, but its status changed during the eleventh century. In 1058, the Jacobite Yahya Ibn Jarir reported that the *Mandylion* was shown just once a year.²³ According to an anonymous Tarragon writer (after 1150),

"[...] the *Mandylion* was always enclosed in a golden vase. And although all the relics were shown to the faithful, the cloth bearing the face of the Lord is not shown to anyone, not even to the Emperor of Constantinople himself."²⁴

The Sack of Constantinople

The separation of the Church into East and West came about during the eleventh century. In 1204, the crusade launched by Innocent III turned into a senseless war between Christians. This ended with the sack of Constantinople when the city was plundered for its valuable relics. An account of the sacking of the city, written by the French knight Robert de Clary,²⁵ emanates wonder at the beauty of what was considered 'the queen of all cities':

"Since the creation of the world, no eye has ever seen nor conquered treasures so great, so magnificent and rich, neither in the reign of Alexander, nor in that of Charlemagne, neither before nor after. Nor do I believe, so far as I know, that the sum of the riches of the forty

Fig. 10 (facing). *Leo VI the Wise bows before Christ Pantocrator*, late-9th century, mosaic from the Imperial Gate; Istanbul, Hagia Sophia.

Fig. 11. *The Conquest of Constantinople*, 1213, mosaic floor, detail; Ravenna, Church of St John the Evangelist.

richest cities in the world amount to those to be found in Constantinople."[26]

Robert de Clary mentions the *Mandylion* and the *Keramion* among the relics of the imperial palace; it is thanks to his eyewitness account that we know where the golden vase, out of everybody's reach, was to be found:

"The palace of Boukoleon was so rich and built in such a style as I will tell you. In this palace [...] there were five hundred rooms, which all connected to each other and were all made of golden mosaic; and there fully thirty chapels both large and small; there was one which was called the Sacred Chapel. Inside this chapel could be found a very rich sanctuary, for they found there two pieces of the True Cross, as large as the leg of a man and as long as a demie toise. And there could be found the iron of the lance which pierced the side of Our Lord, and the two nails which were driven through His hands and His feet. And one found there in a crystal phial quite a lot of His blood, and one found there the tunic which he wore when they stripped him and took him to Mount Calvary...There were also other relics in that chapel which we have forgotten to describe for you. There were two golden vessels hanging in the middle of the chapel from two large silver chains. In one of these vessels, there was a tile, and in the other a large piece of cloth: now we will tell you where those relics came from. A good man was wearing a piece of cloth and our Lord said to him, 'Come, give me that cloth' And the man gave it to him and Our Lord wound it round his face so that his image was imprinted upon it, then he gave it back to him and told him to take it and to allow the sick to touch it, and anybody with faith would be cured of any infirmity. And the good man took it and carried it away, and hid it under a tile until sundown. At sundown, when he was about to go away, he picked up the piece of cloth but as he lifted the tile, he realized that the divine face had impressed itself on the tile as it had done on the cloth; so he took both the tile and the cloth and since then they have cured many of the infirm."[27]

After the fourth crusade, no Eastern Church would claim to possess an image of Christ not made by human hands. The liturgical feast on August 16 was maintained, however, and the Holy Face continued to be the model of Christ's face.[28]

Icon and Relic
Giovanna Parravicini

Fig. 13 (*facing*). *Mandylion* and *Keramion* (facing each other on the drum of the dome), mid-12th century fresco; Pskov, Cathedral of the Monastery of Mirozh.

In the Eastern conception of Christianity, all icons are treated as equivalent to relics, because an icon is painted according to the canons established by the Councils and blessed by the Church, and contains in some mysterious way the presence of the archetype that it represents. This applies most of all to the *Mandylion*, which reproduces "in size and likeness" the linen on which, after touching the Savior's face, His image was miraculously imprinted. The *Mandylion* was considered both a relic, because it had been in physical contact with the Savior's face, and an icon, because it was a portrait of Him.

The authentic portrait of the Savior confirmed the historical reality of His earthly existence in the same way as the remains of the body of a saint does. The *Mandylion* was the basis of the cult of icons and proof of the divine origin of the first Christian image. This was the reason why copies of the relic were widespread, and painters took care to imitate both the linen and the holy face imprinted on it, as well as the way in which it had been preserved, according to the most ancient sources.

Fig. 12. *Mandylion* and *Keramion*, Cod. Ross. Gr. 251, 9th-12th century, f. 12v; Vatican City, Vatican Apostolic Library (from Constantinople).

For example, in the *Account of Emperor Constantine on the Image from Edessa* it is said that King Abgarus had placed the cloth on a table, "adorning it with gold", that is, covering it with a golden exterior. In this way, the linen became invisible, and only the features of the face of Christ remained visible. This way of preserving the relic may be at the origin of the silver and gold adornments on the most important icons.

The most important copy of the *Mandylion* as both an icon and a relic is a miniature painted between the end of the eleventh and the beginning of the twelfth century. It can be found in a Vatican code which illustrates the *Ladder* by John Climacus (Cod. Ross. Gr.251.fol. 12v), where both the *Mandylion* and the *Keramion* (the image miraculously formed on the tile) are depicted next to each other [fig.12]. The idea of the mirror-like arrangement of the two images is reminiscent of the depictions of the *Mandylion* and the *Keramion* which can be seen on the *tympana* of churches, flooded with the light entering through the cupola [fig. 13]. Alexei Lidov, the art historian, suggests that at the origin of the archetype lies the desire to reproduce the space of the niche in Edessa where, thanks to the lamp, the miracle of the duplication of the image took place.[29] This was also probably alluded to by the hanging vessels which contained relics in the imperial palace. An ever-burning lamp assumes the symbolic meaning of theophany of divine light, recalling eternal divine service. The miracle of the image not made by human hands evokes the transubstantiation of bread and wine, which is recalled by the word "victoria" – a reference to Byzantine Eucharistic bread – found on some depictions of the *Keramion*.

"IS THIS THEN WHAT THY FACE WAS LIKE?" THE ROMAN VERONICA

As the man who, perhaps from Croatia, has come to set his gaze on our Veronica, his ancient craving still not satisfied, and who thinks to himself while it is shown: 'My Lord Jesus Christ, God Himself, was this then how You really looked?' [Dante, *Paradise*, Canto XXXI, 103-108]

Fig. 14. *St Veronica with the Veil*, 1450-1460, stone carving, monumental Calvary, detail; Notre-Dame-de-Tronoën, Brittany (photo by Manfred Escherig).

In medieval Europe, everyone was sure that they knew what Christ looked like. Everywhere reproductions of His face could be found, and many of these were considered to be copies of a *sudarium* (a cloth for wiping the face) kept in the Basilica of St Peter's in Rome, on which the portrait of Christ had been miraculously left. This *sudarium* was known as the 'Veronica'.

The *sudarium* became the most famous relic in Rome. Its fame, which was to last over four centuries, started on January 3, 1208, when Pope Innocent III issued a bull establishing a procession on the Sunday after the Octave of the Epiphany. Before this date, there are few references to a *sudarium* that the people call "Veronica" before 1100,[30] and reference to an imprint of the face of Christ upon this cloth appears only towards the end of the twelfth century.[31]

The Sunday after the Epiphany is dedicated to the Wedding at Cana, and Innocent III stipulated that the image of the Savior should be carried "in a reliquary made of gold and silver to be shown to the people gathered to celebrate this wedding with religious devotion."[32] The wedding that the liturgy evokes is that between Christ and His faithful, and the marriage feast strengthens the link that was never to fail between the Eucharist and the Veronica, the contemplation of which was considered to be nour-

Fig. 15. *The Mass of St Gregory*, 1450-1470, oil on panel, detail; Nuremberg, Church of St Lawrence.

ishment for the eyes [fig. 15]. The beginning of the devotion to the Veronica and the spreading of the practice ran parallel to the intensification of popular devotion to the Eucharist, which led to the establishing of the dogma of Transubstantiation and of the Feast of Corpus Domini during the course of the thirteenth century.[33]

The First Indulgence

Matthew Paris, the English abbot and historian, notes in his *Chronica Majora* that in 1216,

"[...] while the Anglian Kingdom was undergoing rather stormy events, Pope Innocent III, concerned that the Church was riding the storm in a rather uncertain fashion, devoutly carried the image of the face of the Lord called Veronica in procession – as is customary – from the Church of St Peter's to the Hospital of the Holy Ghost. At the end of the procession, when it was being put back in its usual place, it turned upon itself so that it was in an upside down position: the forehead was facing the ground and the beard upwards. Horrified by this event, the pope believed that it had happened to him as a sad presage, and in order to reconcile himself fully with God, on the advice of his brethren, he composed a beautiful prayer in honor of the image called Veronica, to which he added a few verses of a psalm and granted an indulgence of ten days to whoever recited it, so that every time it was recited, an indulgence of the same number of days was granted to the person who said it. Many people thus learned the prayer by heart, together with all the verses of the psalm, and made copies of the image so

Fig. 16. Matthew Paris, *Face of Christ in Majesty*, from *Chronica Majora*, c. 1240-1253; MS 26, final sheet of volume 1 (VIIr); Cambridge (England), Corpus Christi College Library.

Fig. 17. Master of Liesborn (circle), *St Veronica Shows her Veil*, c. 1470, Altarpiece of the Passion, detail; Soest, Westphalia (Germany), Hohnekirche.

that greater devotion could inflame their hearts [fig. 16]. It takes the name Veronica from a certain woman by that name, on whose request Christ left his image."[34]

This is the first indulgence linked to an image in the history of the Church. The indulgence could also be obtained before a copy of the Veronica, and this was one of the causes of the immediate spread of the image. From the twelfth century on, through the preaching of St Bernard and later St Francis and St Bonaventure, a new devotion for the Lord's passion was introduced. This manifested itself in deep compassion for the suffering of Jesus. The onlooker's gaze became a crucial factor in the representation of this affection. St Jerome had already written about Christ's gaze:

"If his eyes and face had not held some kind of star-like splendor, the apostles would not have been so ready to follow him, nor would those who wanted to understand his words have flocked to him."[35]

Christ's compassionate gaze is referred to several times in the Gospels: "At the sight of the crowds, his heart was moved with pity for them because they were troubled and abandoned, like sheep without a shepherd."[36] In the dialogue with the young rich man, it is reported that "Jesus, looking at him, loved him."[37] The episode that was commented on most by the Fathers of the Church was Christ's meeting with Peter in Caiphas' house, where his gaze had the power to bring about a change in Peter: "[...] and the Lord turned and looked at Peter; and Peter remembered the word of the Lord, how he had said to him, 'Before the cock crows today, you will deny me three times.' He went out and began to weep bitterly."[38]

This transforming power of Christ's gaze is also attributed to images, as can be seen in Gérard de Frachet's history of the Dominicans, which pre-dates 1269:

"In their cells, they had pictures of the Virgin and her crucified Son before their eyes, so that as they read, prayed and slept, they could look at them, and be looked at by them with compassionate eyes."[39]

The final destination of each person is mirrored in Christ's face. Each one is destined to be like Him, and reaches this through a process of approximation which increases each time one looks on that face. Eyes meet, and starting from a dissimilarity, this meeting of gazes leads one to the eschatological expectation to be like Him, which can be perceived through the diminish-

Fig. 18. Ugolino di Nerio, *Deposition*, c. 1325, tempera on panel, detail; London, National Gallery (originally from the predella of the *Polyptych of Santa Croce*).

Fig. 19. Masaccio, *The Tribute Money*, 1425-1427, fresco, detail; Florence, Santa Maria del Carmine, Brancacci Chapel.

ment of the differences. This is why Gertrude of Helfta (1256-1302) recommended that one should stay continuously in front of Jesus' face, so that once in eternal glory, the celestial court will admire a special similarity with Jesus' face.[40]

The Veronica, being a frontal portrait of Christ, brings about this exchange of gazes between Christ and the faithful more than any other image. Thus it was to be found on the altar retables in numerous churches in Europe, placed at the height of the celebrant's eyes. The art historian Jeffrey Hamburger observes that the first insertions of the Veronica in scenes depicting Calvary seem to have no connection with the sorrowful Passion, but rather respond to the desire to see the relic face to face. Around the figure of Veronica holding out the veil, we can indeed see groups of pilgrims in contemplation [fig. 17] – which is clearly a reference to the display of the Roman relic – arranged so as to create an image within the image, having at its center the serene gaze of a small icon which invites a devotional response.[41] The German mystic, Mechthild of Hackeborn (1241/2-1298), taught her fellow nuns how to undertake a spiritual pilgrimage by reciting an Our Father for every mile separating Helfta from Rome, so as to be able to be present "when the feast of the ostension of the image [took] place."[42]

She was referring to the procession after the Octave of the Epiphany, as was Dante in the *Vita Nuova* (XL, 1), in his mention of the passage of pilgrims through Florence:

"during the season when many people go to see the blessed image that Jesus Christ left us as a visible sign of his most beautiful countenance".[43]

Fig. 20. Workshop of Michel Wolgemut, *Crucifixion*, 1501-1550, tempera on panel, detail; Nuremberg, Germanisches Nationalmuseum.

Fig. 21. Pope Sixtus IV displays the Veronica at St Peter's for the 1475 Jubilee, MS 391, Ludovico Lazzarelli's *Fasti christianae religionis*, late 15th century, f. 41; New Haven, Yale University, Beinecke Rare Book and Manuscript Library.

"He Is Indulgent with Us"
Davide Rondoni
(*translated by Gregory Pell*)

Fig. 22 (*facing*). *The Healing of the Hemorrhaging Woman*, 3rd century, wall painting; Rome, Catacombs of Saints Peter and Marcellinus.

Life seeks out life. We desire not to remain only an image, not to be just ephemeral. But we don't know how. We try to give ourselves more weight, depth – we create things, we accumulate things, we cultivate ourselves, we seek kisses, we invent marvels. In order to enhance ourselves. In order not to feel the lessening of our being. But we don't know how to go about it. "Lovers, if they knew how, could speak marvels in the night. To you, lovers, I ask about us." The ardent poet, Rilke, asks lovers to reveal the secret of that moment in which they seem to touch being itself in an embrace, in the growth of one in the other – but even they are not able. Psychologists call it the absence of / awaiting the other, maintaining the lower-case "o." And in any case, that moment passes. No single deed can add a gram to our existence. No acquisition can give it more substance. Fame? It has no taste. It doesn't enhance us. We build ourselves monuments, at times we reduce others to footstools of our stature. But no rhetoric or inscription increases our "being" one whit. With laser-like acuity, artists like Baudelaire or Pirandello or Conrad, Eliot and others have revealed the hell of our being to the bourgeois society that thought it was thriving by acquiring and basing on itself its own honor of being. Artists are dogs who guard against such falsities. In this era, then, many have preferred to embrace non-being and a vacuous existence that no longer distinguishes between "being and non-being", that no longer has that "problem." Tired of not truly thriving, they've let everything go: they don't build works or ties; culture has become fractured specializations worthy of earthworms, love is no longer even that moment of pure wonder, and every monument is mocked. Yet one face stands out.

"Lift up your face against the beacon that passes
                        [rapidly and cuts down

from the asphalt, I beg you lift your face –
urban tiger,
rare rose in the center of eyes, Indian guide
who places his ear on my heart, on the road
and rises again, and exposes himself to the misfortunes

for we who remain down here, cheek
to the road, the sun gone away,
to feel a bit of warmth that might recall women
                        [to us, the opening
of the door to bars, or certain
summer nights,

leave our faces on the asphalt to have
                        [something similar
to the confidence of the stone
where tears can fall and rest along the cement,
                        [very slow
the kisses

...

My gracious captain, who suffers ever after
on every front

I look at your hand
cutting a piece of fruit, to touch

the hair of one wounded to death
or to brush it from the eyes
of the one I love...

If I were not yours, I would be
only words, high gorges
where delirious the day faithfully follows
                        [the night –

hold me among your own, those who alone or
[in droves
seek the hill where stories are murmured and
[at times one sings
with a light of the dawn among broken voices..."

(Davide Rondoni)

He offers us indulgence, for our hunger, our restlessness. He indulges our being and our near non-being. The face of He who is. We look at Him, and we can receive indulgence and strength. He mends what in us continually unravels. Would that He finally ennobled us.

Fig. 23. *Emperor Vespasian Healed by Veronica's Veil*, c. 1510, Brussels tapestry; New York, Metropolitan Museum.

Veronica, the Bleeding Woman

Piety and, above all, devotion to the Passion, were nourished by meditating on the mystics, on mystery plays, and on apocryphal works or sources which were neither canonical nor official, but whose accounts and teachings were edifying for the soul, leading to greater love and generosity. In this vibrant context, an answer was found to the desire to know the story of the woman named Veronica – on whose initiative (according to the prayer by Pope Innocent III), the Lord left his image imprinted on a cloth, as a memory.[44] For reasons that still remain unclear, Veronica began to be associated with the story of Bernice, the woman healed by Christ of an issue of blood, according to the apocryphal Pilate Cycle.

The *Acts of Pilate* deal with Jesus' trial. The earliest form of these *Acts*, dating from the second or third century, were later known as the *Gospel of Nicodemus*. In the course of Jesus' trial, many people healed by Jesus testify, including a woman called Bernice, who turns out to be the woman cured by Jesus of long-term bleeding.[45] Since she was a woman, her testimony was contested by the Jews present, and then disregarded totally. At that point in the trial, Veronica (Bernice) disappears from the scene.

In the work entitled *Cura Sanitatis Tiberii* (The Healing of Tiberius), dated the fifth or sixth century, Veronica was given a more important role. Having painted a portrait of the Lord, she was taken to Rome to cure Emperor Tiberius of leprosy. In *The Savior's Vendetta*, published before the year 900, the origin of the portrait is said to be miraculous, as Jacobus de Voragine narrated in the Golden Legend (1264-1298):

"My lord and my master when he went preaching, I absented me oft from him, I did do paint his image, for to have alway with me his presence, because that the figure of his image should give me some solace. And thus as I bare a linen kerchief in my bosom, our Lord met me, and demanded whither I went, and when I told him

Fig. 24. *Procession to Calvary*, 1480, sculpture in polychromed and gilt wood, altar, detail; Arle, East Frisia (Germany). Church of St Boniface.

whither I went and the cause, he demanded my kerchief, and anon he emprinted his face and figured it therein."[46]

The memory of Bernice or Berenike, the bleeding woman, is recorded by Eusebius, who wrote that in Paneas (Caesarea Philippi), in front of Berenike's house, he had seen a bronze statue of a kneeling woman next to a standing figure, presumed to be Jesus. In the West, this same woman is associated with Lazarus' sister, Martha,[47] whereas in Spain, she is curiously associated with Marcella, Martha's servant girl. Following the account of Veronica in Rome, after Tiberius had been healed, she remained and died there, and her tomb could apparently be seen in the old basilica of St Peter's, while in the French legends, St Veronica married Zaccheus, and travelled with her husband and St Martial to Provence, in France, where she died in a hermitage around the year 70. She was buried in Bordeaux, where her ancient Merovingian tomb can still be seen.[48] All these variations on the same theme testify to the interest all over Europe in the woman who was mentioned in Innocent III's indulgence prayer.

From the twelfth century on, we find the first attempts to insert Veronica's compassionate gesture in the context of the Passion, as if the authors of the time, inspired by the accounts of crusaders and pilgrims to the Holy Land, were trying to find a more important occasion for it. In 1147 Pietro Mallio re-echoed the hypothesis that the image was imprinted on the veil by Jesus' sweat in the Garden of Olives.[49] In France, in the *Chanson de Geste* Veronica is afflicted by leprosy and draws near to Jesus on the cross and brushes His face with her veil. The oldest version of the episode where Veronica wipes Jesus' face on the way to Calvary can be found in *Joseph d'Arimathie*, written by Robert de Boron in 1191:

"I happened to have made a linen cloth and was carrying it to market where I hoped to sell it, when I met the people who were leading the prophet through the streets, his hands bound, followed by the Jews. And he asked me to wipe away the sweat that was running down his face. So I took one end of the cloth at once and wiped his face; then I went on my way and the Jews led him on, flogging him. And when I got home and looked at the cloth, I found this image of his face. That's exactly how it happened."[50]

The account of the meeting between Veronica and Christ on the way to Calvary reached its definitive form with Roger d'Argenteuil in

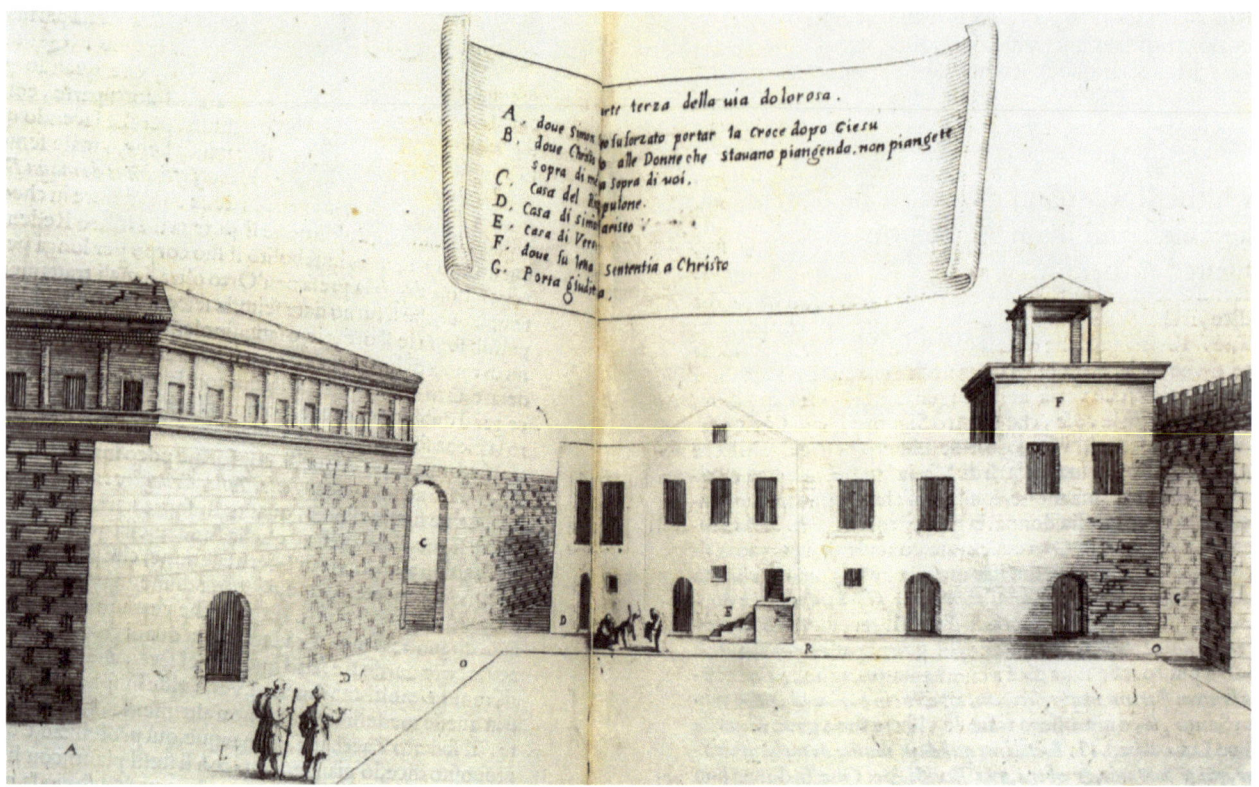

Fig. 25. Jacques Callot, *Third Station of the Cross* (R1v and R2r), in Bernardino Amico OFM, *Plans of the Sacred Edifices of the Holy Land,* Florence, Pietro Cecconcelli alle Stelle Medicee, 1620; Jerusalem, General Library of the Custody of the Holy Land.

1300.[51] According to the new sentiments inspired by St Francis, Christ's gift was no longer the Son of God's answer to Veronica's desire (or King Abgarus') to see him, but became the Redeemer's reward for the compassionate gesture of a woman who loved him to the point of jeopardizing her life for him.

In the same period as Roger d'Argenteuil, we find the first reference in Jerusalem to the place where Jesus apparently gave the image of his face on the cloth. It was only in the middle of the fifteenth century that the place where Christ met Veronica was identified, as a station of the *Santo Circolo* (Holy Circle), an itinerary organized for pilgrims by the Franciscans in Jerusalem. The place was identified as the threshold of an Arab house, which is symbolized on pilgrims' maps by a small staircase [fig. 25].[52] Therefore, while the tradition in Paneas regarding the bleeding woman, Veronica, is ancient, the record of Veronica in Jerusalem is ten centuries' later.

Throughout the 1100s, these texts claimed no link with Rome or Roman relics. To date, there are no written accounts of pilgrims who went to St Veronica's tomb in Rome or the *sudarium* before 1200, when an English pilgrim, Gervase of Tilbury, visited Rome. He observed that the venerated portrait did not have a prodigious origin, but that Veronica had commissioned the portrait from a painter, and that subsequently the painting was associated with her name.

Fig. 26. Lombard School, *St Veronica with the Veil,* c. 1280, fresco; Hoè Superiore (Lecco), Church of St Veronica.

Towards the end of the thirteenth century, Gerald of Wales added the etymology of Veronica as "true icon" (a word coming partly from a Latin root, and partly from a Greek one, *vera* + *eikon* = true image): *Vera icona, id est, imago vera.*[53] This etymology has enjoyed good fortune, but historians consider it highly unlikely that a medieval anagram should be at the root of such a widespread and venerated figure.

At present, the oldest representation of St Veronica with the veil is dated 1280. It is a fresco in a church with the same name in Hoè Superiore, in the province of Lecco, Italy [fig. 26]. From the first Holy Year (1300) on, the figure of the Veronica was to spread throughout Europe.

The Holy Years

On February 22, 1300, Boniface VIII instituted the first Holy Year from the "past festivity of Christmas",[54] which was to see "an immense, countless gathering of people who came to obtain the plenary indulgence."[55] In *De Centesimo seu Jubileo Anno liber*, written in the Pope's honor during the same Jubilee year, Cardinal Iacopo Stefaneschi narrates how the Holy Year came about, with the unusual flocking of pilgrims which began on the evening of January 1.[56] The cardinal recounts that the Pope was at the Lateran Palace and the day passed without any extraordinary events:

"And the astonishing thing is this: for almost the whole day on January 1, the secret of the new remission remained hidden; but as the sun went down, towards evening, and almost in the total silence of midnight, the Romans came to hear about it, and behold, they came running in crowds to the holy basilica of St Peter's. They crowded round the altar, getting in each other's way, so that it was almost impossible to get close to the altar, as though they thought that by the end of that day, which was drawing to a close, the grace would have been exhausted, or at least most of it."[57]

Fig. 27 (*facing*). Giacomo Grimaldi, *Boniface VIII Shows Himself to the Crowd from the Loggia of the Blessings in the Lateran,* late 16th century, water-coloured drawing on paper; Milan, Biblioteca Ambrosiana.

Stefaneschi reports that both Roman citizens and foreigners continued to come to Rome in great numbers for about two months, in "groups that were more numerous than usual on the days when the whole world could see the venerable image, called the *Sudarium* by the people, or the Veronica."[58]

It was these crowds of people which convinced the Pope to make the bull "retroactive" from February 22. The bull did not cite the Roman relic, but on a parchment kept in Cortona, Tuscany, drawn up by the Papal scribe, Sylvester, the text of the bull is reproduced and clarified. For example, it explains the term Jubilee, which is not present in the institutional bull.[59] One detail which makes the parchment unique is a miniature, in the upper and lower margins, of the Face of Christ, placed between standing figures of St Peter and St Paul [fig. 28]. These images are meant to show the last stages of the pilgrimages to be carried out in the Jubilee year. In order to obtain the indulgence, the Bull indicated that it was necessary to visit the tombs of St Peter and St Paul, but the culmination of the pilgrimage was to see the imprint of the face of Christ on Veronica's veil. As Giovanni Villani wrote:

"For the pilgrims' consolation, every Friday and every solemn feast day, the Holy Face is displayed in the Vatican basilica."[60]

Card. Stefaneschi described the great agitation and clamor which began after the publication of the Bull:

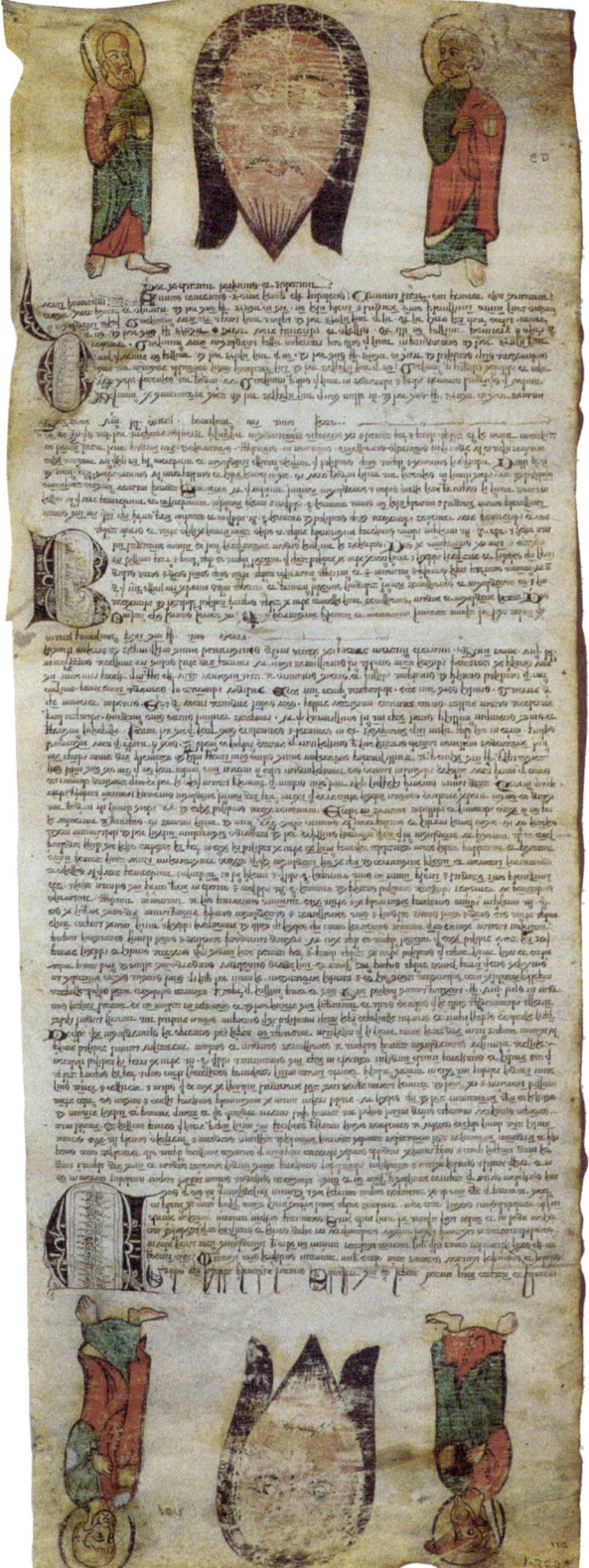

Fig. 28. *The Holy Face between St Peter and St Paul,* Letter by Papal scribe Sylvester, 1300; Cortona, Library of the City and of the Etruscan Academy.

Fig. 29. Pilgrims in Rome for the Jubilee of 1300, from the *Chronicles of Giovanni Sercambi*, illumination; Lucca, State Archive.

Fig. 30. *St Veronica with the Holy Face*, 15th century, pilgrim badge, lead; Vatican City.

"Through the regions of Italy, Hungary and Germany, as word spread like wildfire about the pardon to be accorded once in a century, crowds of people set off in an instant, in droves, towards Rome, so numerous as to resemble an army or a swarm of bees."[61]

The sensation that something extraordinary was happening was shared by all the chroniclers of the time. Such huge crowds had never been seen "so that it seemed incredible to anyone who didn't see it."[62] One such chronicler, Villani, tried to express it in terms of quantity, claiming that "in the whole year in Rome there were over two hundred thousand pilgrims, apart from the Romans, not counting all of those coming and going on the roads." There were also women, children, and the sick, who were all rarely seen on pilgrimages:

"husbands, wives and children left their houses boarded up and all together went with perfect devotion to the proclaimed pardon [...] elderly people of seventy years old or more and the infirm on litters [...] and many young people, having no money, carried their fathers and mothers on their shoulders or their backs [...]. A dense crowd gathered inside and outside the walls of the city, getting larger and larger as the days passed, and many were crushed in the throng."

Stefaneschi points out that "a second gate was opened in the walls to afford the pilgrims a shorter path."

Dante refers to the crowds walking in both directions on the bridge of Castel Sant'Angelo:

"just as, because the throngs were vast the year
of Jubilee, the Romans had to find a way
to let the people pass across the bridge,
so that all those on one side face the castle,
heading over to Saint Peter's,
these, on the other, heading toward the mount."[63]

The destinations of this movement of peoples

Fig. 31. Andrea di Bonaiuto, *Triumph of the Church Militant*, 1366-1367, fresco, Cappella degli Spagnoli, detail; Florence, Santa Maria Novella.

Fig. 32. *St Veronica with Veil*, c. 1410, Parish Church of St Blaise; Ravecchia (Bellinzona), Ticino.

were the Basilicas of the Apostles, the last of which was the great Constantinian Basilica of St Peter's, its façade decorated with mosaics commissioned by Leo I and Gregory IX. From the square, bordered by oratories and chapels, after climbing thirty-five steps, the pilgrims arrived at the great quadriportico with the famous pine cone in the middle of the courtyard. On the stairs, under the colonnade and under the *Navicella* mosaic (showing Christ saving St Peter and the Apostles from the waves), the *pictores Veronicae* – the Veronica painters – sold reproductions of the Veronica. The outer walls were crowded with stalls where pilgrims could buy 'veronicas', which were badges made of tin or lead which showed that they had been on the threshold of the tombs of the Apostles. In the same way as the shell and the cross were symbols of pilgrims going to Santiago and Jerusalem, these badges became symbols of the journey which was rewarded by the vision of the face of the Lord. [figs. 30-31]

Fig. 33. *Exposition of the Holy Face*, from Stephanus Planck's *Mirabilia Urbis Romae*, c. 1486, woodcut.

The five doors and the huge basilica cannot have been big enough to contain the "vast crowd", according to the pilgrims' accounts. One can almost relive the terrible day when an English monk, William of Derby, was crushed and mortally wounded by the crowd pressing to see the Veronica.[64] Although the crowds reduced the time one had to see the relic to just a few moments, the desire to see it did not diminish, nor did the emotion and admiration of the pilgrims. Dante describes this in canto XXXI of *Paradise* (103-108):

"As the man who, perhaps from Croatia,
                                            [has come
to set his gaze on our Veronica,
his ancient craving still not satisfied,
and who thinks to himself while it is shown:
'My Lord Jesus Christ, God Himself,
was this then how You really looked?'"

From 1300, the Veronica became the image that was most copied around Christendom, and the most famous relic in Rome. The Holy Face, shown graciously by St Veronica, became a recurring motif along the pilgrim routes of Europe. A publication that acted as a sort of guide for pilgrims, called *Mirabilia Urbis Romae* (The Wonders of the City of Rome) [fig. 33] and published in 1375, reported that those who were present at the display of the Veronica could obtain an indulgence of one thousand days if they lived in Rome, six thousand if they came from nearby, and twelve thousand if they came from afar.

Fig. 34. Andrea di Bonaiuto, *Triumph of the Church Militant*, 1366-1367, fresco, Cappella degli Spagnoli, detail; Florence, Santa Maria Novella.

Fig. 35. Tiberio d'Assisi, *St Francis Proclaims the Indulgence for the Pardon of Assisi*, 1518, fresco, Chapel of the Roses; Assisi, Basilica of Santa Maria degli Angeli.

The hymn *Salve Sanctae Facies* (Hail, Holy Face) is attributed to John XXII (1316-1334), who was resident in Avignon. An indulgence of ten thousand days was granted to those who recited this hymn in front of a copy of the Veronica. The hymn, which describes the transfigured and luminous face of Christ on a cloth given to Veronica as a sign of love, spread far and wide.[65]

Petrarch went to Rome for the Jubilee of 1350. Similarly to Dante, when referring to the Veronica, he emphasizes the individual pilgrim's desire to see the face of the Lord:

"Grizzled and white, the old man
leaves the sweet place where he has provided
[for his life
and leaves the little family, filled with dismay

Fig. 36. Parmigianino, *Veronica between St Peter and St Paul*, 1524-1527, ink and watercolour, square grid; Florence, Uffizi, Department of Prints and Drawings.

that sees its dear father failing it:
He reaches Rome following his desire
to gaze on the image of Him
whom he hopes to see again in heaven."66

There was a lively debate in the 1300s regarding the moment when the blessed would be able to see God. The resolution was found in 1336 by Benedict XII, who anticipated the beatific collective vision of the end of all time to a personal encounter when the soul leaves the body of the single person at the moment of death.67 This is the context in which the texts by Dante, Petrarch and the *Salve Sanctae Facies* hymn were written, which we can imagine being sung by scores of pilgrims to Rome in front of the relic:

"Hail, our joy,
in this hard life,
fragile, fleeting
and soon everlasting.

Oh happy figure,
lead us to the end,
that we may see
the face of Christ."68

The pilgrim's loving gaze at the Veronica was experienced as an anticipation of the moment in which Christ and the soul meet face to face.

The crowds attracted during the Holy Years continued in the following centuries. In the *Memoriale del Giubileo del 1450* (Memorial of the 1450 Jubilee), by Paolo di Benedetto, it is noted that "the guilds that made the most money were the following: first of all the bankers and pharmacists and painters of the Holy Face, these made a great deal, and next were the inns and taverns."69

The Holy Face painters, whose stalls were situated around St Peter's Basilica, obtained a licence to sell Veronicas from the Record Keepers of the Chapter of St Peter.

For the Jubilee of 1525, Ugo da Carpi was commissioned to do an altar painting for the Veronica altar in St Peter's. He asked his friend Parmigianino for a preparatory grid drawing, which he followed exactly except for the face of Christ. This he drew with a dark countenance and without a crown of thorns [figs. 36-37]. In his *Lives of the Artists*, Vasari writes

"Ugo da Carpi was a mediocre painter, but nonetheless a genius for wonderful inventions. And since, as I said, he was a painter, I will not hide the fact that he painted a canvas that is in Rome at the altar of the Holy Face with oil,

Fig. 37 (*facing*). Ugo da Carpi, *Veronica between St Peter and St Paul*, c. 1525, altarpiece; Vatican City, Historical Archive of the workshop of St Peter's.

Fig. 38. Venetian School, medieval frame of the Veronica, 14th century, wood, rock crystal, enamels; Vatican City, Treasury Museum of St Peter's Basilica.

but without a brush, using his fingers and other strange instruments. One morning when I was at Mass with Michelangelo at that very altar, having seen that it was signed by Ugo da Carpi, I showed the signature to Michelangelo, laughing. He too laughed, and said, "it would have been better if he had used a brush, and if he had done it in a better manner." You can still read the inscription today on the canvas: done by Ugo da Carpi wood-cut engraver, without a brush."[70]

This painting could be the last copy of the Veronica that Dante and Petrarch saw.

What Was the Veronica Like?

Considering the crowds of pilgrims who arrived in Rome to see the relic, and the numerous copies made of it, it might seem surprising that we know little of the appearance of the Veronica other than its size, which we can deduce from a cracked frame [fig. 38] made of rock crystal. This frame for the Veronica – the largest slab of rock crystal in existence – was donated by three Venetian noblemen during the Jubilee of 1350 "because of their special devotion to the holy sudarium, which is preserved in the basilica and displayed for the consolation of sinners and the remission of sins."[71]

It is difficult to make a definite "identikit" of the Roman Veronica because of the great divergence between the copies made of it.

Dark and Luminous

By instituting the procession around the time of the Epiphany, Innocent III linked the relic to

Fig. 39. *St Veronica with the Veil*, Arundel MS 302, English Book of Hours, c. 1450, f. 163; London, British Library.

Fig. 40. Anonymous Austrian painter, *A Family Praying before the Veronica*, c. 1490, oil on panel; Sarasota, Florida, Museum of Art.

the manifestation of Christ rather than the Passion. Thus, until the mid-1400s, there are no representations of the Veronica on the way to Calvary. Nonetheless, while the face of Christ is serene and has no signs of suffering, in some copies the face is luminous, and in others it is dark, bluish, or almost black. Since the hymn *Ave Facies Praeclara* (Hail, Most Noble Face) says that the face of Christ is darkened by suffering (*anxietate denigrata*), while in another hymn *Salve Sanctae Facies* (Hail, Holy Face) the luminous beauty of the face is praised,[72] it has been hypothesized that the colors of the face were linked to one or the other hymn. Karl Pearson[73] discards this hypothesis and observes that the versions with the bluish face are normally associated with *Salve Sanctae Facies* which should underline luminosity.

Others maintain that the versions with the darker face, which is however not suffering, are copies of the *Mandylion*; the rather rigid contours of these Veronicas that seem to suggest the invisible frames around icons would reinforce this hypothesis [figs. 41-43]. What is not convincing about this is the fact that dark Veronicas are found geographically close to the Roman relic itself, the last of which is that of Ugo da Carpi, on the very altar on which the Veronica was kept. The idea therefore that the dark face derived from the *Mandylion* would only make sense if the original Veronica was identical to the *Mandylion*.[74]

Fig. 41. *St Veronica with the Veil between St Peter and St Paul*, c. 1430 fresco, altar frontal; Manta, Cuneo (Italy), Monastery-Church of St Mary.

Fig. 42. *Holy Face*, copy of the Roman Veronica, c. 1376; Jaén, Cathedral of the Assumption.

Fig. 43. Anonymous Roman painter, *Golden Veronica*, copy of the Roman Veronica, c. 1368, tempera on linen fiber paper; Prague, Treasure of the Cathedral.

Fig. 44. *The Holy Face of Laon*, c. 1200, Slavic icon; Laon, Cathedral.

In this sense, a Byzantine influence on the copies of the Veronica – like all Western art from the twelfth and thirteenth centuries – can certainly be hypothesized. The parchment in Cortona, which is the oldest extant copy of the Veronica (and a particularly important one because of its nearness to the enigmatic original) describes an object that is similar to the extant copies of the *Mandylion* in its serene frontal face, which seems to be surrounded by an invisible frame, with the hair centrally parted and with a pointed beard. Even Giacomo Grimaldi, in his book (*Opusculum*) on the Veronica, states that all these portraits resemble each other.[75] In fact, in several cases, copies of the Veronica are confused with copies of the *Mandylion*, and vice versa. We will now list a few.

In 1249, the abbess of the convent at Montreuil-en-Thiérache asked her brother in Rome, the future Pope Urban IV, for a copy of the Veronica; what she received was a magnificent copy of the *Mandylion*, with the inscription in Paleo-Slavic "portrait of the Lord on Mandylion" [fig. 44].[76] In the accompanying letter, the Pope asks her to welcome it "like the holy Veronica, as its true image and likeness."[77] The Holy Face in Jaén [fig. 42], a copy given to the Bishop of Jaén, Nicola de Viedma, by Pope Gregory XI (who had returned to Rome from Avignon in 1377), is considered to be a copy of the *Mandylion* in the Church of San Silvestro (Rome), an icon that is probably Byzantine in origin, now kept in the Vatican.

On the other hand, the copies of the Veronica (the *Golden Veronica* [fig. 43] and the *Sad Veronica*) which the Holy Roman Emperor Charles IV took back to Prague after his visit to Rome in 1368, were wrongly considered to be copies of the *Mandylion*, by Karl Pearson. Indeed, he could not understand the reasons for their name in relation to the Veronica.

Another example of the identical iconography of the two *acheiropoieta* can be found on the list of relics from Constantinople which were bought at great cost by King Louis IX of France, who built the Sainte-Chapelle in Paris specifically to house them. The main relic was the Crown of Thorns, but in the list there was also "sanctam toellam tabulae insertam" (a holy towel inserted in a frame) which is thought to be the *Mandylion*, or a copy of it. It is curious to see how its name changes on the inventories through the years, becoming a *Véronique* from 1534.[78] From the registers, we can also learn that the material appeared to have deteriorated and only maintains the "appearance of an image"[79] so it might have been a copy of the *Mandylion* that arrived in Paris, and not the original relic, but it is not possible to verify this because the treasure of the Sainte-Chapelle was dispersed during the French Revolution.

Fig. 45. Robert Campin, *St Veronica with the Veil*, c. 1420, oil on panel; Frankfurt, Städelsches Kunstinstitut.

Fig. 46. *The Holy Face*; Manoppello (Pescara), Shrine of the Holy Face.

If the Veronica had been dark, and hard to distinguish from its background in the same way as an icon, as it would seem from the accounts of copies in Jaén and by Ugo da Carpi, the descriptions of it as being bright and luminous would be incomprehensible, as would the many copies of it which reproduce a fair-colored countenance. Another hypothesis can be made starting from Luther's description of the Veronica, on his visit to Rome in 1511: "It is simply a square black board, on which a transparent piece of cloth hangs and above this there is another veil. There poor Jena Hans cannot have seen anything more than a piece of transparent cloth that covers a black board. This is the Veronica which is shown."[80]

46

Fig. 47. *The Holy Face*; Manoppello (Pescara), Shrine of the Holy Face.

Fig. 48. *The Holy Face*; Manoppello (Pescara), Shrine of the Holy Face. The same side as in the previous image, illuminated only frontally.

As a matter of fact, a thin, almost transparent veil can produce different effects according to what it is placed against. This can be seen with the veil of Manoppello: if you look at it frontally against the light, the image becomes literally invisible [fig. 46]. If it is placed against something light-colored, a light-colored face with well-defined features becomes visible; if placed against a dark background, the color of the flesh barely emerges and only the white of the eyes are well-defined.

As a final note on the luminosity or darkness of the image, which are the features that create the most perplexity among critics (and which are therefore normally kept distinct), it must be noted that they were already well known in the thirteenth century. In her description of the Veronica in 1289, well before the hymn *Salve Sancte Facies* was composed, Gertrude of Helfta (later known as St Gertrude the Great) put the enigmatic dark color and the luminous brightness together, explaining that, just as in Christ there is both the passion and the resurrection, his humanity and his divinity, so is the Veronica both human and divine, dark and bright.[81]

In the same way, a century later, the English mystic Julian of Norwich mentions changeability as a characteristic of the relic in St Peter's, referring to it as "the Holy Vernacle at Rome, which He hath portrayed with His own blessed face when He was in His hard Passion, with steadfast will going to His death, and often

changing of color", characterized by "diverse changing of color and countenance, sometimes more comfortably and life-like, sometimes more ruefully and death-like."[82]

These apparently contradictory descriptions would not be enigmatic if the Veronica were similar to the Veil of Manoppello. Indeed, according to the way it is lit, the Holy Face in Abruzzo either appears bright and serene or suffering and dark [figs. 47-48].

Bloodied and Crowned with Thorns

As mentioned previously, the aim of the first inclusion of the Veronica in scenes from the Passion was not to describe the moment of the miraculous impression of the face on cloth. Indeed, it is only from the end of the fifteenth century that we find copies of the Veronica in which Christ's face carries signs of suffering, the crown of thorns and drops of blood.

Christ began to be depicted wearing the crown of thorns, both on the Veronica and in Crucifixion scenes, after the relic of Christ's crown had been taken to Paris in 1239 by Louis IX.[83] Typically, the color of the crown was bright green, which was another act of homage to that particular relic. It was introduced as an iconographic detail starting from the description made of it by Nicholas Mesarites,

Fig. 49 (*facing*). Antonio da Tradate, *Christ Meets the Veronica*, 1490, fresco; Palagnedra, Ticino, Church of St Michael.

Fig. 50 (*top*). Master of the Strauss Madonna, *Imago Pietatis with Mary and Mary Magdalene*, c. 1400, panel painting; Florence, Galleria dell'Accademia.

who pointed out that the crown was still fresh and green, not faded in the least.[84] It is interesting to note an artistic reluctance to paint the crown of thorns on Veronica's veil: for a long time, we can see Christ crowned with thorns leaving Veronica his suffering portrait without the crown of thorns. This reluctance might indicate that artists had an authoritative prototype to follow, which had no crown of thorns. And in fact, there are no versions that claim to be copies of the Roman relic which include the crown of thorns.

It is also noteworthy that, despite the value attributed to the suffering of Christ by medieval piety (think, for example, of the image of the *man of sorrow*), facsimiles made before 1500 of Veronica's *sudarium* which are streaked with blood are rare. One example is the iconography of the *Imago Pietatis*,[85] in which Christ's body, covered in blood and framed by the symbols of the *Arma Christi* (Instruments of the Passion),[86] is offered to the faithful for their compassion. At the same time, Christ's face in the foreground is resplendent with light on Veronica's veil [fig. 50].

The Cult of the Veronica in Illuminated Manuscripts

Silvana Tassetto

Illuminated manuscripts offer precious evidence of the great desire to see and know the true face of Christ to a greater extent. This desire had been rekindled both by the prayers and indulgences linked to the Roman Veronica, and the institution of the Jubilee years.[87] Until 1400, this Face was mostly radiant and bore no signs of the Passion; it was a frontal image which analogically referred to the mystery of the Eucharist, not only from an iconographic perspective,[88] but also because of its position within texts (placed near the Canon, for example). One significant example of this can be found in the encyclopedia, *Omne bonum*, compiled in London by the clerk of the Exchequer, James Le Palmer, around 1360-1365.[89]

In this book, the Holy Face appears three times. On folio 15, it is placed among the Instruments of the Passion, and is followed by the hymn *Ave Facies Praeclara* (Hail, Most Beauteous Face) and by the suggestion that an indulgence can already be obtained by contemplating the *imago pietatis*. On folio 16 and 16v, it provides a comment to the themes of the beatific and salutary vision of God [fig. 51], taking the form of a large face, with a beard divided according to the type of the Roman Veronica. It is spherical on fol.16, like a consecrated host, and is a half-bust on the other two occasions, like the prototypical English illuminated manuscript *Chronica Majora* by Matthew Paris[90] [fig. 16]. A second example can be found in the missal from the Benedictine abbey Church of St Mary the Virgin (also known as Sherborne Abbey) from the beginning of the fifteenth century. On fol. 279, which corresponds

Fig. 51. *Adoration of the Holy Face*, MS Royal 6 E VI, vol. 1, *Omne bonum*, 1360-1375, f. 16v; London, British Library.

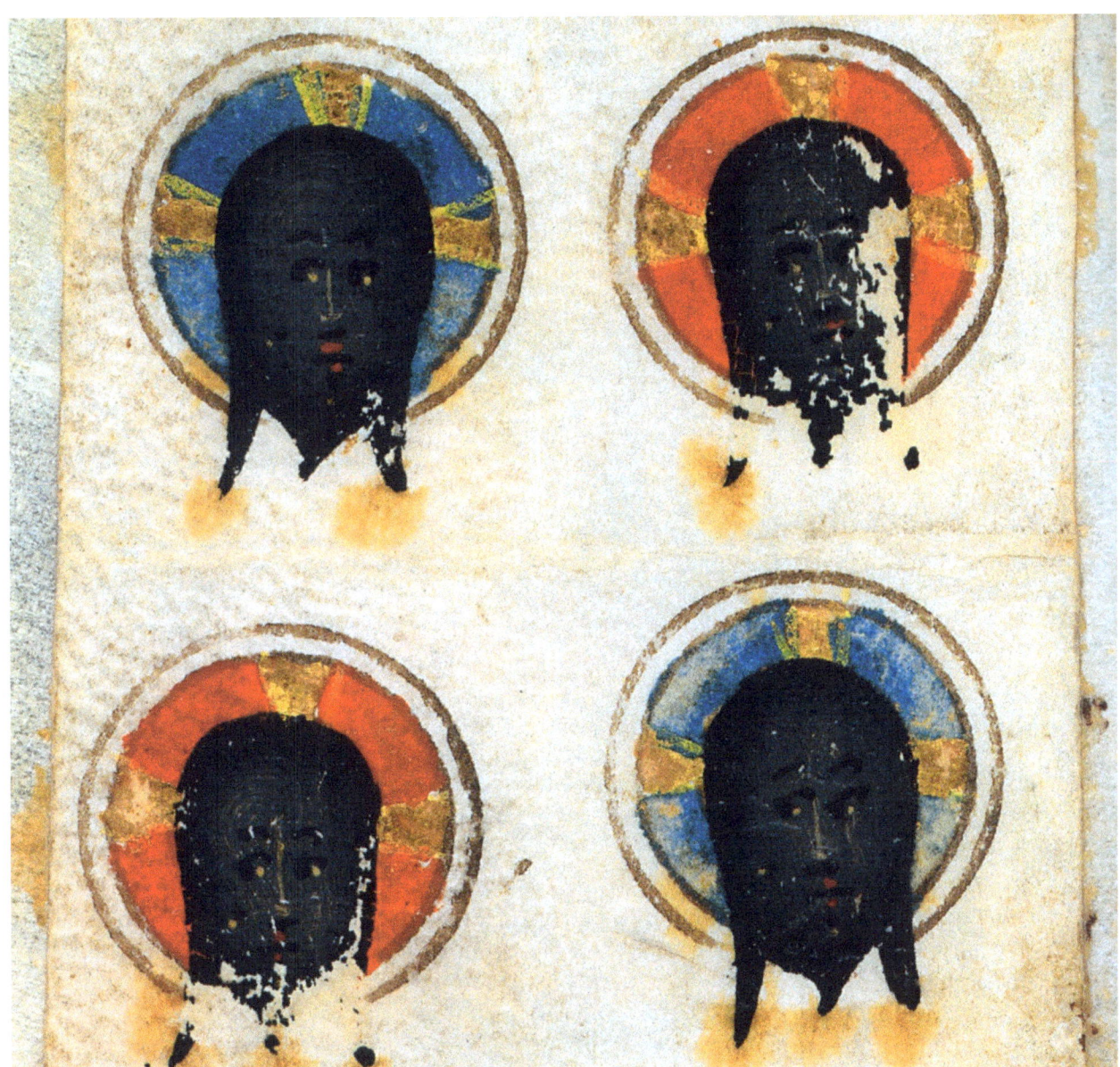

to the feast of *Corpus Domini*,[91] in the C of *Corpus* at the top, a celebrant is drawn in the act of distributing the Eucharist, and immediately underneath it, within the D of *Domini* there is a small representation of St Veronica, almost totally bending over, opening her arms wide as she holds up the white veil with the imprint of the Holy Face. On the left, Abbot Bruynyng, the patron, is kneeling in deep devotion before this beatific vision, inviting the onlooker to pray and take part in the same experience. A third example is the series of small Veronicas [fig. 52] painted on leather or parchment, which were often sewn

Fig. 52. *Four Veronicas*, MS Thott 117, German Cistercian Psalter, second half of the 15th century (unbound sheet inserted between cover and first page); Copenhagen, Det Kongelige Bibliotek.

near the prayer of the Canon and placed in the books for private or monastic prayer.[92] For lay people, they were like souvenirs, having been used as badges during pilgrimages to Rome.[93]
The Holy Face imprinted on a veil was reminiscent of the Byzantine tradition of the *Mandylion*.[94] However, in the iconography of the Veronica, it is rare to find only the *sudarium*. It is more often found held up by angels or between Saints Peter and Paul, as a memory of a pilgrimage to Rome,[95] [fig. 28]. When referring to a Jubilee year, it can also be found being held by an acolyte, as in the illuminated manuscript with Pope Sixtus IV [fig. 21] which shows the Veronica in St Peter's during the Jubilee of 1475. In this case too, the image which is placed over the altar acquires a strong Eucharistic significance.[96]
From the fifteenth century on, the Veronica is found almost exclusively in Books of Hours, and in prayer books used by both religious and the laity. Some are very simple, others very refined, some fabricated for Popes or royals or their dignitaries by the most important artists of the time.[97] In the prayer books, the Office of the Veronica[98] was accompanied by a copy of the image of the Holy Face, and started with prayers of supplication taken from Psalms 4:7 and 67:2, followed by the prayer written by Pope Innocent III, the hymns *Ave Facies Praeclara* and *Salve Sancta Facies,*[99] normally with a premise explaining the indulgence linked to the prayers. The veil is almost always depicted as being held by St Veronica, the intermediary, who holds up the Holy Face and looks at the reader, inviting them to participate in the gift she received. She is often dressed in clothes of Eastern origin, in reference to the hemorrhaging woman, Berenice, with whom she is associated in the oldest books, such as a beautiful Book of Hours from Flanders.[100]
In Italy, religious practice has always been more choral and communitarian, rather than intimate, as in the rest of Europe. This is perhaps the reason why, even though the Veronica was held in Rome, votive practice found greater fortune beyond the Alps (in the Franco-Flemish regions, but also in the Netherlands, Germany and England), undoubtedly because of the private pietistic devotions promoted by the movement entitled *Devotio moderna*.[101] Northern art in the 1400s, through its strong realism of sacred images, seems intent on answering the need for an individual relationship with God through prayer. It becomes a kind of dialogue in which the world of the person praying becomes one with the object of devotion. This can be seen in the half-bust representations of Christ, which correspond to his physical description provided in the apocryphal letter written by the procurator Publius Lentulus to the Roman Senate, which was used as a source by many artists of the time.[102]
Up until 1400, no matter the source and the iconographic variant associated with it, Christ's face was always depicted without signs of suffering. It is only after that date that the litanies of Veronica are added to those of the Passion, and in the Divine Office, an image of sorrow, or of Veronica accompanying Jesus on the way to Golgotha, begins to appear beside the hymn *Salve Sancta Facies,* which mentions a transfigured face.[103] An example of this can be seen in a Flemish Book of Hours printed at the beginning of the sixteenth century, where Christ helps St Veronica show his suffering and merciful face, while carrying the cross [fig. 53].[104]
This change was echoed in religious processions and plays, and is undoubtedly linked to the spread of the mendicant orders, particularly the Franciscans, who emphasized the suffering humanity of Christ in their preaching.

Fig. 53 *(facing). Veronica with Veil on the Way to Calvary*, MS Ludwig IX 18, by the Master of James IV of Scotland, Book of Hours, 1510-1520, f. 8v; Los Angeles, Paul Getty Museum.

The *Opusculum de sacrosancto Veronicae sudario* by Giacomo Grimaldi

Paola Francesca Moretti

Giacomo Grimaldi (1568-1623)[105] was a canon of St Peter's Basilica in Rome. His work concerning the Veronica is one of the most precious sources about the story of the relic in Rome. The *Opusculum*, currently unpublished, is preserved in three autograph manuscripts, one of which dates from 1621 and is preserved at the Ambrosiana Library in Milan.[106] The *Opusculum* is a lengthy document – the Ambrosian manuscript is 183 pages long – and is decorated with a large number of illustrations by the author himself. Grimaldi's source is acknowledged by one of his contemporaries, an erudite cleric of the same Basilica, Tiberio Alfarano.

The story of the Veronica told by Grimaldi is perhaps too coherent and consistent. The Veronica was taken to Rome in the year 34; it was kept in the ancient Constantinian Basilica of St Peter's from the time of its construction (fourth century); it was preserved in a ciborium (also defined as *altare* or *sacellum*) built by Pope John VII in 705; in 1606, it was transported to the so-called "Veronica pillar" under the dome of the new Basilica of St Peter, built by Pope Paul V. Its story ends, according to the *Opusculum*, in 1617, when Pope Paul V prevented painters from copying the Veronica without his permission, many copies having been made of it.

Grimaldi's chronological account is based on many different sources, both ancient and modern. It is worth noting that he often seems to write in the tone of an apologia, as if he were asserting the truth of his account against readers who distrusted it.

The great amount of historical and archeological data he lists should be examined and evaluated in

Fig. 54. Giacomo Grimaldi, *Opusculum de sacrosancto Veronicae sudario*, MS H. 3, dated 3 May 1618, title page; Vatican City, Archive of the Chapter of St Peter's.

detail, which is why it would be worth making a critical edition of the monumental text. Just one example of Grimaldi's mistakes will be cited here. Grimaldi devotes ten pages of his work to the description of the *sacellum* where the *sudarium* lay until 1606, but recent researchers have discovered that the *sacellum* was not built by Pope John VII, nor does it date from 705. Although there are still scholars who accept the date of 705,[107] it has been ascertained that the *sacellum* was erected by Pope Celestinus III (1191-1198), and that an inscription bearing the name of John VII was reused for it (hence, the misleading date of 705).[108]

Last but not least, we cannot guess why Grimaldi, whose work is full of detailed pictures (designs of

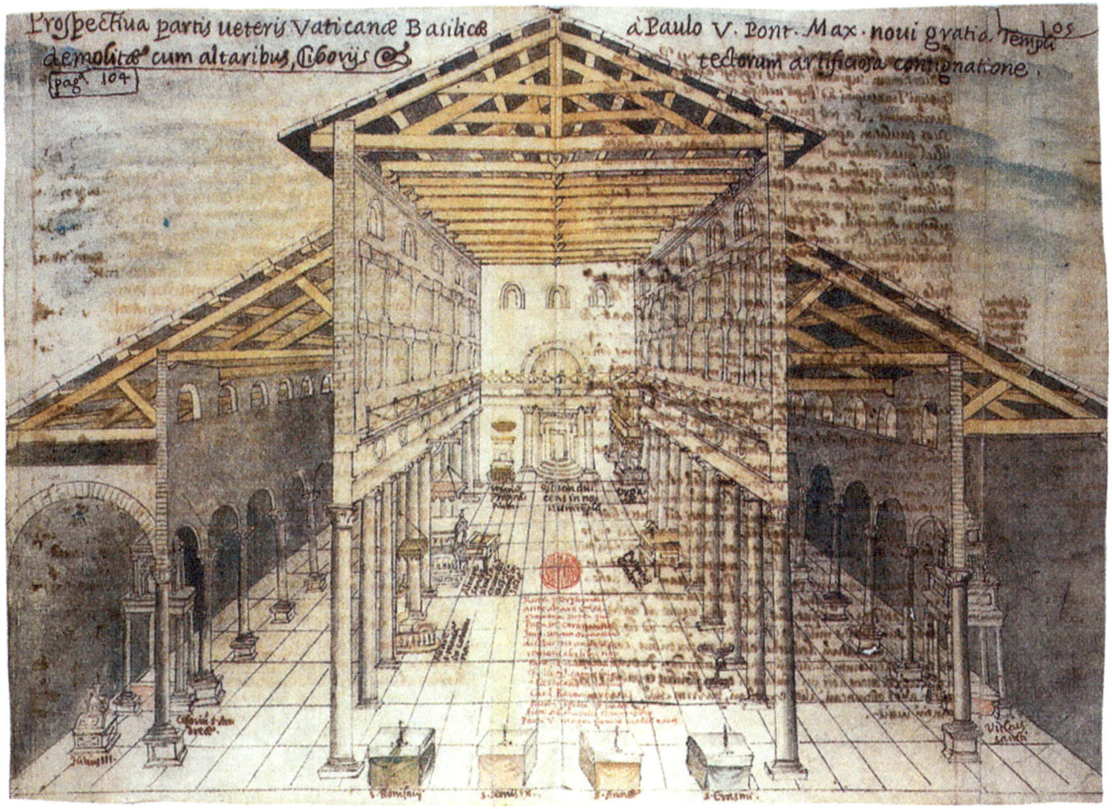

Fig. 55. Giacomo Grimaldi, *Interior of Old St Peter's Basilica*; the Veronica ciborium is in the right-hand aisle.

Fig. 56. Giacomo Grimaldi, *Ciborium of the Veronica*, drawing from *Opusculum de sacrosancto Veronicae sudario*.

the interior of the Basilica, mosaics, inscriptions, relics, the *sacellum* itself), has not painted any picture of the Veronica.[109] Even in the frontispieces of the autograph copies of the *Opusculum* we find nothing but a portrait of Christ which can be described as stylized, in that it does not have any special features that might recall the other images of the Veronica.[110]

"MEN HAVE LOST A FACE"
THE MODERN ERA

"Mankind has lost a face, an irretrievable face, and all have longed to be that pilgrim – who in Rome sees the Veronica and murmurs in faith, "Lord Jesus, my God, is this then what Thy face was like?" [Jorge Luis Borges, "Dreamtigers"]

There are two events in the sixteenth century that mark the history of Rome and the story of the Veronica: the construction of the new basilica of St Peter's, planned by Julius II and started in 1506, and the sack of Rome in 1527.

In 1506, "Pope Julius began to build a huge construction, proud, worthy, broadening it with admirable columns, and wondrous and extremely costly vaults."[111] On April 19 the first stone of the new basilica was laid. In fact, it was on the spot where one of the four columns would be placed, the one that was to be called "the Veronica pillar", being destined to contain the most important Roman relic. Work started with the demolition of the basilica presbytery, which had been built twelve centuries previously by Emperor Constantine the Great. The demolition was immediately the cause of great controversy. Given the considerable costs of the new building, Pope Julius II declared in two separate bulls, published on February 12 and November 4, 1507, that anyone who contributed alms for the sake of the new basilica could obtain an indulgence. The "sale" of indulgences, as it was erroneously called, was not the real cause of what was to be the most se-

Fig. 57. Graffiti of 1527 on Raphael's *Triumph of Religion* (or *Disputation on the Blessed Sacrament*); Vatican City, Vatican Palace, Stanza della Segnatura.

Fig. 58. Giovanni Balducci called the Cosci, *Jesus Meets Veronica on the Way to Calvary*, 1594-1596, fresco; Rome, Basilica of St Prassede.

rious crisis of the Western Church, but it was certainly one of the pretexts.

The Sack of Rome 1527

On May 6, 1527, the mercenary soldiers of Charles V of the Habsburgs conquered Rome. The culmination of the pillage of the city was the looting of sacred objects and relics. Hearing the news that Rome was at the mercy of the imperial army, all of Europe feared that the Veronica, the most important relic, might have suffered a despicable fate. A letter to the Duchess of Urbino written by her representative, Urban, dated May 21, 1527, reads, "some say even the Veronica has been burnt...The Holy Face has been stolen and passed through a thousand hands, and has by now been through all the taverns in Rome..."[112]

In one account, a Landsknecht affirms, "in all the churches, St Peter's, St Paul's, St Lorenzo's, and even in the small ones, chalices, chasubles, ostensories and ornaments were taken and, not having found the Veronica, the looters took other relics."[113]

People soon began to report that the *sudarium* had been miraculously saved. In his *Opusculum*, Giacomo Grimaldi noted that he had heard from some officials at the basilica who had witnessed the sacking that the Veronica, the Spear and St Andrew's head had remained unharmed. The keys to the case of the *sudarium* had been lost,[114] so that in 1528, new ones had to be made for the sum of 10 *carlini* (coins). He summed up the situation and the wondrous survival of the relics thus: "God blinded their intellect so that they could not stretch out their evil and sacrilegious hands on such precious relics."

The relic had certainly been put back under Paul III, because apart from the Ostensions recorded for Holy Week in 1533, all the chronicles of the time report that at the end of his stay in Rome, on April 16, 1536, Emperor Charles V was able to venerate the Veronica like any other pilgrim.[115]

The showing of the Veronica continued after the Council of Trent, which attributed great importance to relics and images. During the Holy Year of 1575, for example, the Veronica attracted more than 400,000 pilgrims to Rome from all over Europe.[116]

At the same time, however, a new, distant attitude could be seen towards the Veronica, first of all in Roman circles.[117] In the Sistine Chapel, Michelangelo chose not to include Veronica's Veil among the instruments of salvation grasped by the gigantic angels in his Last Judgment, and he depicted Christ with features inspired by an ideal of beauty. In 1582, at the request of Cardinal Baronio, St Veronica was removed from the official list of martyrs,[118] and

Fig. 59. Frans Francken, *St Veronica Offers her Veil on the Way to Calvary*, 1622, oil on panel; whereabouts unknown.

Fig. 60. Federico Zuccari, *Christ Meets St Veronica*, 1595, oil on slate, Olgiati Chapel altarpiece, detail; Rome, Basilica of St Prassede.

Fig. 61 (*facing*). Polidoro da Caravaggio, *Christ's Way to Calvary* (preliminary drawing for the *Capodimonte Altarpiece*), 1534, oil on panel; Rome, Palace of the Chancellery.

Charles Borromeo removed her from the Ambrosian calendar and Breviary.[119] The suppression of Veronica did not involve the *sudarium*, which was considered "an inexhaustible source of graces."[120]

The most striking novelty, however, regards the artistic representations of the Veronica: in the post-Tridentine era, artists were invited more than ever to represent Veronica's veil, but what they produced were ideal, intuitive versions that were clearly not linked to one model.

Particularly among artists living near Rome, we can find three different styles, which differed considerably from the past in the way in which the meeting between Christ and Veronica was represented [figs. 59-61]. First of all, there is a tendency to depict the moment preceding the impression of Christ's face on the veil; secondly, while in previous centuries the veil had been spread out in front of the eyes of the onlooker, like a miniature ostension, it was now held up by the woman in such a way that it was impossible to see any image. Lastly, Christ's face was shown like an indistinct bloodstain.[121] We can find a description with details that tally with this in *Viaggio in Italia (Journey to Italy)* by Michel de Montaigne, which is quite possibly the last chronicle of an ostension in the old St Peter's Basilica:

"In these days the Veronica is being shown; an emaciated face, dark and gloomy in color, in a square as big as a mirror; it is displayed with great solemnity from a high pulpit, about five or six paces wide."[122]

Later, the Spanish artist Francisco de Zurbarán did a series of paintings of Christ's face, in which his features were increasingly evanescent [fig. 62].

In January 1606, because of work on St Peter's, the Veronica was transferred to an iron cask in the basilica's archive. On the evening of March 21, 1606, it was placed in the "Veronica" pillar in the new St Peter's.[123] Pope Paul V asked Giacomo Grimaldi to collect all possible information about the Veronica and the other major relics so as not to lose anything about their history. Placed on high under the grandiose cupola of St Peter's, together with the Sacred Spear, the fragment of the True Cross, and the head

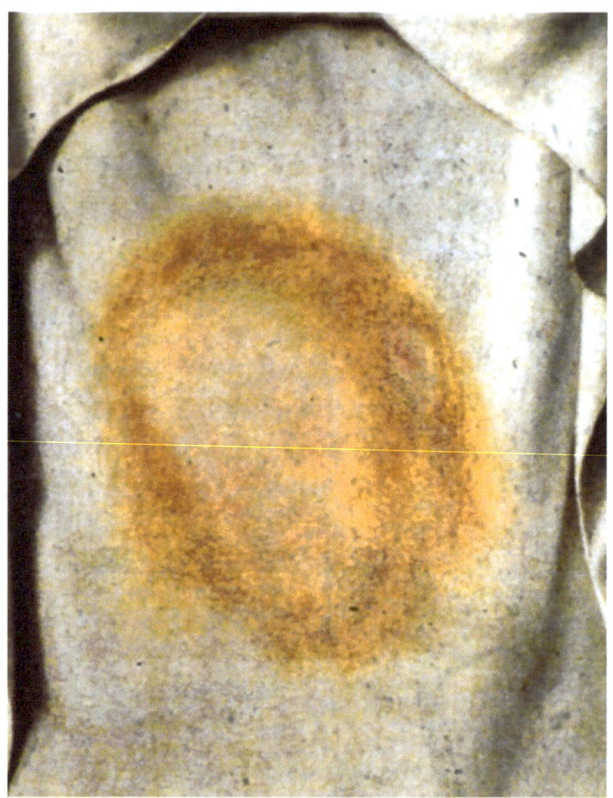

Fig. 62. Francisco de Zurbarán, *The Holy Face*, 1658, oil on canvas; Valladolid, National Museum of Sculpture.

of St Andrew, the Veronica received definitive confirmation of its importance, but its physical reality fell into second place, and it ceased to be the object of pilgrims' exclusive and impassioned devotion. The three major relics of the Passion, high up among the columns supporting the dome (the symbol of Christ's passion which sustains the Church) invite the faithful to lift their eyes to Heaven.[124]

A New Veronica?

In 1615, the imperial court at Vienna asked Pope Paul V for a copy of the Veronica for Queen Constance of Poland. The request was an embarrassing one for the Pope, and it took him

Fig. 63. Pietro Strozzi, *Veronica's Face Veil* 1617, linen cloth; Vienna, Palace Hofburg, Schatzkammer.

Fig. 64. Pietro Strozzi, *Veronica's Face Veil*, 1621, copy of the Roman Veronica donated by Pope Gregory XV to the Duchess Sforza; Rome, Church of the Gesù.

a year to send a copy of the relic, made by Pietro Strozzi, one of the canons in St Peter's [fig. 63]. The Pope apologized for the delay in sending it, blaming it on the difficulty of finding a good painter among the canons, who were the only people who were allowed access to the relic. It can be deduced, therefore, that the copies made by the *pictores Veronicae* (Veronica painters) were not considered reliable.

The copy painted by Strozzi introduces a considerable break from the traditional Veronica face: Christ is depicted with His eyes closed, as though already dead. This profound and inexplicable difference is the main cause of skepticism regarding the Roman relic. Grimaldi, a canon, notes in his booklet *Opusculum* that the image is faithful to the relic that he saw in 1606 and that Strozzi made five more before Paul V, in the very moment when he sent the image to Vienna, prohibited other copies from being made, under pain of excommunication.

Looking at these copies, one might ask why Strozzi did not even respect the proportions of the face indicated by the golden frame surrounding it [fig. 64]. If the reason were that, out of good faith, he preferred to obey what he saw rather than what he knew, the difference from the old copies of the Veronica could be explained by the swapping of the original with a copy during the sixteenth century. According to this hypothesis, if watercolors (the only type of paint which can give the impression of not being painted) began to naturally fade on the counterfeit cloth, they might have created

Fig. 65. Marco Benefial, *The Instruments of the Passion Presented to the Virgin Mary*, 1721, coal and graphite on cardboard, detail; Rimini, City Museum.

forms that Strozzi interpreted as closed eyes and a big mouth. It is quite likely that Strozzi was also inspired by the features of the face on the Holy Shroud of Turin. If Paul V had not known about the substitution, his embarrassment would have been caused by the deterioration of what was boasted of as a marvel of Christendom, whose prodigious origin was demonstrated precisely by its capacity to last through time.[125]

Seeing that there were widespread requests for the Roman relic, Pope Paul V's prohibition to make copies of the Veronica (later confirmed by Gregory XV) remains enigmatic. In 1628, by means of a letter sent by Cardinal Spada, Urban VIII ordered that all copies of the Roman Veronica be handed in to the local parish priest or bishop on pain of excommunication. In a second letter, dated July 15, 1628, the same cardinal, "in order to soothe the consciences of those who misunderstood the prohibition" specified that "it was not the intention of His Beatitude to forbid anyone from keeping images, other than those that represent the true Sacred Image of the Holy Face that can be seen here in the Basilica of St Peter's, with stains, and bruises, marks of sweat and blows; in other words, the image of the Savior, which is also called 'Holy Face' by some of you."[126]

Traces of these measures can be found in parish registers. For example, in the Church of Santa Maria Vergine ad Armeno on Lake Orta, Bishop Volpi, during a pastoral visit in 1629, ordered a fresco showing Veronica and the *sudarium* to be whitewashed.[127]

Once the niches by Bernini within the columns designed by Michelangelo were finished, along with the balconies designed for the exposition of relics,[128] on April 20, 1629, Urban VIII "venerated the Holy Relics with great devotion and admired them with spiritual satisfaction, forbidding on pain of excommunication, of which he had a notice erected, that anyone should move the veil covering the Holy Face, or open the vase containing the Holy Spear, without pontifical approval."

From this moment on, showings of the veil at a height of twenty meters made the Veronica practically invisible to the faithful.

In artistic works, there are a few sporadic re-ferences to the copy of the Veronica made by Strozzi. Between the end of the 1600s and the beginning of the 1700s, there are a certain number of Veronicas which became contact relics, because of contact with the *sudarium* from Rome, in which Christ has his eyes open and shows signs of suffering.

In 1742, Benedict XV encouraged parish priests to spread devotion to the *Stations of the Cross*: in this way, Veronica's compassionate gesture, which is remembered in the sixth station, was welcomed back into churches once again.

Fig. 66. On June 7, 1897, a seriously ill and feverish Thérèse of Lisieux, poses with the images of the Child Jesus and the Holy Face.

The Holy Face between 1800 and 1900

Devotion to the Holy Face revived unexpectedly during the nineteenth century in France, thanks to a young Carmelite from Tours, Marie de Saint-Pierre. The work of Sr Marie is linked to the Veronica because of the words that Jesus spoke to her, "Seek out Veronicas who will dry and adore my divine face, adored by only a few people."[129] A lawyer named Léon Dupont became the driving force behind this movement, and he chose a printed copy as his version of the Holy Face, inspired by Strozzi's copy of the Veronica, which had become a contact relic of the Veronica in St Peter's. In 1885, Louis Martin enrolled in this Arch-confraternity, together with his daughters, the youngest of whom would later be raised to the altars as St Teresa of the Child Jesus and of the Holy Face [fig. 66].

No scientists believed in the authenticity of the Holy Shroud of Turin when, in 1889, the lawyer Secondo Pia photographed it for the first time. The negative created a very strong impact [fig. 67]. Alongside the aristocrats from Turin, a French doctor by the name of Paul Vignon rushed to see the plates. Back in France, Vignon made the images known to his friends, including the painter Georges Rouault, who subsequently painted the Holy Shroud and the Veronica many times [fig. 68]. Thus in this era, which appeared to go through a third iconoclastic crisis,[130] there was an increase in news and attention centering on Christ's Face.[131]

Fig. 67. *The Holy Shroud*, detail of the negative image of the face; Turin, Cathedral.

Fig. 68. Georges Rouault, *The Holy Face*, 1933, oil on canvas; Paris, Musée National d'Art Moderne.

Fig. 69 (*facing*). *Veronica's Pillar*, 1606; Vatican City, St Peter's Basilica.

It is significant that the Church accepted and encouraged research on the Holy Shroud, but has acted differently as regards the Veronica.[132] Even today, it is extremely difficult to have access to the relic, and photographs of it are forbidden.[133] One of the few scholars allowed access to it, Joseph Wilpert, after removing two panes of glass that protect it, wrote that it was "a square piece of light-colored material, rather faded with time, with two indistinct rust-brown stains on it, joined together."[134]

In 1945, the Italian mystic, Maria Valtorta, wrote that Jesus had left the imprint of his face on Veronica's veil as a comfort for his mother, and that the image would goad skeptics:

"You who proceed via dry tests, O rationalists, you who are luke-warm, or waver in faith, compare the face of the *Sudarium* and that of the Shroud. One of them is the face of a living man, the other the face of a dead man. But the length, breadth, somatic features, form, features are the same. You will see that they correspond."[135]

Valtorta's work was published with a note referring to the relic kept in St Peter's,[136] but the Roman relic contradicts this description, because it is indecipherable and therefore cannot be measured.[137] Furthermore, if Strozzi's copies are accurate, the Roman relic depicts a dead man like that of the Shroud, and not a living man, as the mystic asserted. On the other hand, Valtorta's description matches the veil of Manoppello, but it does not seem that she knew anything about the image kept in the Abruzzi region. Also in the diaries of a young Portuguese woman, Blessed Alexandrina Maria da Costa, there is a reference to the "lasting" quality of the linen of the Veronica, saying "that matchless portrait will be contemplated until the end of time."[138]

On the occasion of the Jubilee Year in 2000, the Biblioteca Apostolica Vaticana and the Palace of Exhibitions organized a large exhibition entitled *The Face of Christ*. The section in the catalogue dedicated to the Veronica closes by raising the question of what really is conserved in the column [fig. 69] in St Peter's.[139] In the introduction to the same volume, Card. Jorge M. Mejía states that St Peter's Basilica "once housed Veronica's Veil",[140] hinting at its loss or transportation elsewhere, which would confirm the widespread opinion among critics that the veil probably disappeared during the sack of Rome in 1527.[141] The Holy Face would thus seem to be definitively lost.

But Pope Benedict XVI, by choosing to visit Manoppello at the beginning of his pontificate, brought attention back to the Holy Face, "whose mysterious gaze does not cease to rest on men and women and all peoples."[142]

Fig. 70. On 1 September 2006, Benedict XVI kneels in prayer in Manoppello before the Holy Face.

"AN ETERNAL IMPRINT"
THE VEIL OF MANOPPELLO

Clio [that is, history] passes her time seeking imprints, vain imprints, and an ordinary Jewish girl, little Veronica takes out her handkerchief and from Jesus' face takes an eternal imprint. That's what throws everything up into the air. She was there, in the right place at the right time. [Charles Péguy, 1912]

In the first half of the 1600s, when the Abruzzi region was part of the Kingdom of Naples, attention was drawn to an image imprinted on a veil, in the small city of Manoppello. The veil depicts the living face of Christ, which carries visible marks of violent blows. It cannot be explained how the veil was made. The face does not seem to have been painted, and is clearly visible to the same degree on both sides of the veil.

The image belonged to the doctor Donato Antonio De Fabritiis, a well-known gentleman in the region, who decided to bequeath it to the Capuchin friars in Manoppello in 1638. A few years later, the Capuchin preacher Donato da Bomba wrote a *Relatione historica* (an historical account), which recounted the vicissitudes of the veil up until that point.[143] Moreover, the *Relatione* placed the image alongside other images of Christ not made by human hands, including the *Mandylion* from Edessa, the Roman Veronica and the Shroud. From the earliest record of it, therefore, the face of Manoppello

Fig. 71. Manoppello (Pescara), Procession of the Holy Face on the third Sunday in May.

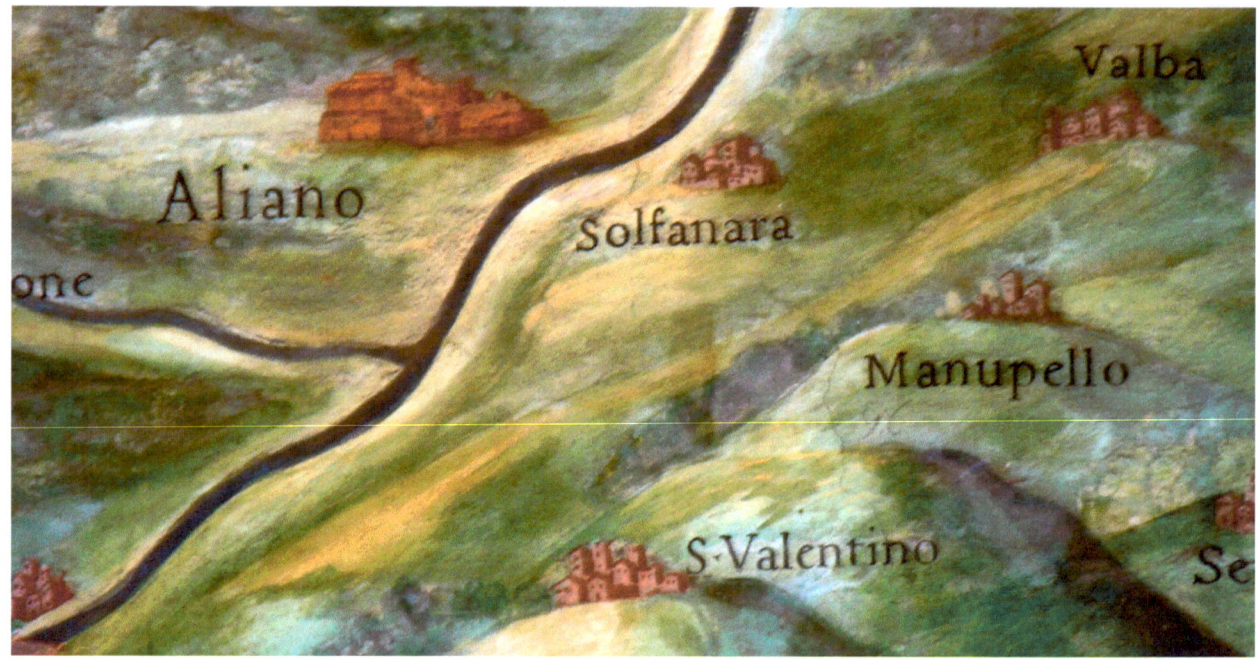

was considered to be sacred and was placed among other *acheiropoieta* (images not made by human hands).

The Arrival of the Veil

The *Relatione Historica* recounts the story of the arrival of the relic in Manoppello and contains some elements typical of legendary hagiographic narratives.

"In the time of Julius II the Roman Pontiff, about the year of our Lord 1506, during the time of Maximilian III of the Austrian emperors [...] there lived in Manoppello, a very civilized, well situated land, having all things necessary for rich and abundant human living, in the region of Abruzzo, Province of the said Kingdom of Naples, the very famous Giacomo Antonio Leonelli, doctor in medicine, astrology and other liberal arts... One day Giacomo Antonio Leonelli was in the public square just outside the door of the mother Church of said town of Manoppello, the title of which is St Nicholas of Bari, in honest conversation with other peers, and while they were speaking a pilgrim arrived unknown by anyone, with a very venerable religious appearance, who having greeted this beautiful circle of citizens, he said, with many terms of manners and of humanity to Dr. Giacomo Antonio Leonelli that he had to speak with him of a secret thing which would be very pleasing, useful and profitable for him. And thus, taking him aside just inside the doorway of the church of St Nicholas, gave him a parcel, and without unfolding it told him that he ought to hold this devotion very dear, because God would do him many favors, so that in things both temporal and spiritual he would always prosper.

Giacomo Antonio took the parcel, and turning on the one hand towards the holy water font began very deftly and secretly to open it. And seeing that it had the most sacred image of the face of Our Lord Christ, he remained at

Fig. 72 (facing). Ignazio Danti, *Map of Abruzzi*, 1580-1585, fresco, detail; Vatican City, Vatican Museums, Gallery of Maps.

Fig. 73. Donato da Bomba, *Relatione historica*, copy dedicated to the Minister General of the Capuchin Order; L'Aquila, Provincial Archive of the Capuchin Friars. The copy is kept together with its 1646 authentication certificate.

first quite frightened, bursting into most tender tears, which he stopped then (so as not to show this to his family friends), and thanking God for such a gift, picked up the image. He turned to the unknown pilgrim to thank him, to bring him to his home and to show him pleasantries, courtesies and gratitude, but did not see him anymore. Remaining even more shaken than before, though only exteriorly (because interiorly he was filled with extreme spiritual joy), the very adventurous Leonelli, almost stuttering, inquired of his fellow citizens about him, who all affirmed that they had seen him enter with him into the Church but not exit.

Whereupon full of wonder, with the greatest diligence he sought him and had him sought within and without Manoppello, also throughout the countryside, sending a number of persons through the many streets and paths, and yet it was impossible to either see or find him, hence all judged that that man in the form of a pilgrim to be a heavenly angel, or else a saint from Paradise."[144]

According to the *Relatione Historica*, the veil remained the property of the Leonelli family for nearly a century, until in 1608 the soldier Pancrazio Petrucci, husband of Marzia Leonelli – a descendant of the medical doctor Giacomo Antonio – violently appropriated it, after a quarrel with his wife's relatives regarding the division of the inheritance. Years later, Pancrazio was incarcerated for reasons unknown to us, and finding himself in need he wrote to his wife to sell the veil: Marzia sold it to Donato Antonio De Fabritiis for four *scudi*. This happened in 1623 according to one source,[145] or in 1618 according to another.[146] At first De Fabritiis did not

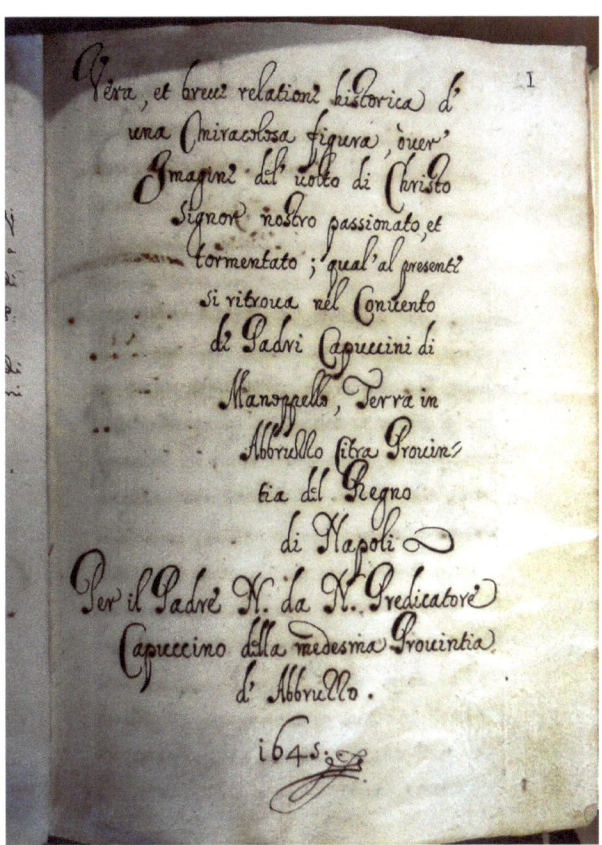

realize the value of the object he had acquired, especially because the veil, badly maintained by Marzia and Pancrazio, was "all ragged, torn and worn and moth-eaten",[147] but when the doctor showed it to the Capuchin friar Clement da Castelvecchio, the friar grasped its extraordinary nature and urged De Fabritiis to keep it. Indeed, after trimming the outer border of the veil that had frayed, the friar carefully cleaned it himself. In addition, De Fabritiis, "eager to delight in the most holy image with greater devotion," placed it in a wooden frame with crystal glass on both sides, decorated with a walnut

Fig. 74. Since 1703, on the Feast of the Holy Face, the veil has been carried in procession from the shrine to the town of Manoppello.

frame and woodwork by a [...] Capuchin friar named Brother Remigio da Rapino" which is the case in which the veil is found to this day.[148]

Thus we come to the donation of the veil to the Capuchins and to the *Relatione Historica* in which the donation is spoken of. In April 1646, a document was drawn up on parchment by the notary Donato De Donati in Manoppello. In this document, sixteen local witnesses certified the truth of the facts narrated in the account by Donato da Bomba.

Even if some parts of the narrative seem to be rather romanticized, this does not mean that the account by Donato da Bomba does not also contain historical facts. In fact, the historical research undertaken reveals exact correspondence, confirming the existence of all the persons cited, as living in the late 1500s and early 1600s. There remains only to unravel the identity of a "Giacomantonio Leonelli" living in the sixteenth century, who would be the one who received the veil from the stranger "with a religious and very venerable appearance." From the end of the 1600s, the devotion to the relic began to spread, without ever reaching great fame, however. For a long time, the veil of Manoppello remained the patrimony of local piety, although it also became known to ecclesiastical scholarship.[149]

The silence was broken on May 31, 1999, when Father Heinrich Pfeiffer, professor at the Gregorian University, outlined a revolutionary hypothesis in a conference at the foreign press association in Rome – that the Holy Face of Manoppello is none other than the Roman Veronica, and that the Holy Face in Abruzzo is probably the ancient *Kamouliana*.[150]

The Historical Authenticity of the *Relatione*: Verifications and New Data

Arianna Petraccia and M. Cristina Terzaghi

The Franciscan monastery of Manoppello was built around 1300 by Napoleone Orsini, Prince of Guardiagrele. The church was dedicated to St Lawrence, the Martyr. Manoppello remained the feudal property of the Orsini family until 1495, when Pardo Orsini's domains in Manoppello passed into the hands of Fabrizio Colonna, later succeeded by his son, Ascanio. The Colonna family remained attached to Manoppello and its church, and maintained the right to appoint chaplains of their own patronage in the parish of San Pancrazio up to the seventeenth century. In the State Archives of Naples and of Chieti, there are several unpublished early seventeenth century documents which concern the Franciscan establishment in Manoppello. They attest to the generous donations from Donato Antonio de Fabritiis and his family for the re-establishment and expansion of the Capuchin monastery, construction of which began in 1620. It was Donato Antonio who gave the veil with the Holy Face to the convent of Manoppello, according to the *Relatione Historica*. Donato Antonio was the son of Baron Fabrizio, was born in 1588 and married Claudia Cianti in 1613. They had two children, Giovanni Antonio and Costanza. The documents confirm the account of the *Relazione*: Donato Antonio de Fabritiis was a devout and respected man, who held the position of Prior of the Confraternity of the Most Blessed Sacrament during the years 1607-1608. He was particularly devoted to the friar Andrea Rocca di Botte, who was considered an extremely holy man when he died in the convent in 1651. Indeed, Donato kept his eyeglasses as a relic. According to the *Relazione*, Donato Antonio bought the veil from a certain Marzia Leonelli, who was constrained by need to cede it to him because of the incarceration of her husband Pancrazio Petrucci. The unpublished documents provide some information about Marzia and her husband. Born in 1588, Marzia was probably the daughter of Giovanni Nicola Leonelli (1517-1607), and is likely to have married Pancrazio Petrucci in 1606, their first son, Giovanni, being born in 1607. They had two more children, Sabia Veronica Letizia, born on October 30, 1610, and Ascanio on September 29, 1616. Pancrazio Petrucci was a military man and, in all likelihood, a prominent public figure. Of great interest is a notarized document drawn up on April 17, 1622 in which the two spouses declare they have received goods belonging to Marzia's deceased uncle, Giacomo Antonio Leonelli, which were temporarily in Marzio's Leonelli's possession. This news tallies remarkably with the *Relatione Historica* according to which Marzia inherited the veil, of which Giacomo Antonio Leonelli was the first owner. It is thus possible to prove a family relationship between Marzia and Giacomo Antonio Leonelli and the passing of goods from one to another. However, it is not easy to establish whether this Giacomo Antonio is the same protagonist of the *Relatione*. If we hypothesize that he was the brother of Giovanni Antonio, Marzia's father (1517-1607), he would have been more or less the same age. However, he could also have been a great-uncle, who had actually received the veil in 1506, as stated in the *Relatione*. In any case, it must be pointed out that the Act of Donation, which attests to the authenticity of the relic, is less clear about the date of the arrival of the veil in Manoppello. Marzia Leonelli died on February 4, 1643, and this allows us to suppose that the *Relatione* was drawn up previous to that, since the text states that at the time Marzia was still alive. Incidentally, February 4 is the feast of St Veronica; a coincidence perhaps, but a particularly extraordinary one for someone who had loved that mysterious veil so much.

The Copies of the Historical Account
Michele Colombo

The *Relatione historica* (historical account) by Donato da Bomba has come down to us in several copies, and different editions. The autographed original, which, according to Filippo da Tussio, was kept in the Capuchin convent in Vasto,[151] cannot apparently be found, because of the instability caused by the earthquake of 2009. Nonetheless, there are four extant codices from the 1600s. Three of them are kept in L'Aquila, in the provincial archives of the Capuchin Friars, and the last is in the archives of the Capuchin Friars in Manoppello. Two of the codices from L'Aquila, dated 1645, were transcribed by Ambrogio da Pescara, a Capuchin friar. The first, which bears the name of the author Donato da Bomba, must have originally been in Manoppello, since it has an accompanying letter drawn up by the Provincial Father Silvestro dalla Fara (dated Chieti, September 30, 1647) which gives permission for the manuscript to be "kept in the same place as the most sacred image of the Holy Face." At the bottom of the manuscript, there is also a note recalling a plan made in 1703 to replace the glass panes of the reliquary which held the Holy Face, and the abandonment of the plan when it was noted that one of the panes was stuck to the veil. In the second manuscript, kept together with its authentication by the notary Donato De Donati, dated 1646 [fig. 73], the *Relatione* is curiously defined as being carried out "by Father N. from N., Capuchin preacher." The dedicatory letter to Innocenzo da Caltagirone, the General Minister of the Capuchin friars, is signed in the same way, "N. from N.", on pages 3-4. The first and last pages of this manuscript contain historical notes about the *Relatione*, written in different hands, which can be dated to the 1600s and the 1800s.[152]

It would seem that the third copy of the *Relatione* in L'Aquila can be identified as that previously kept

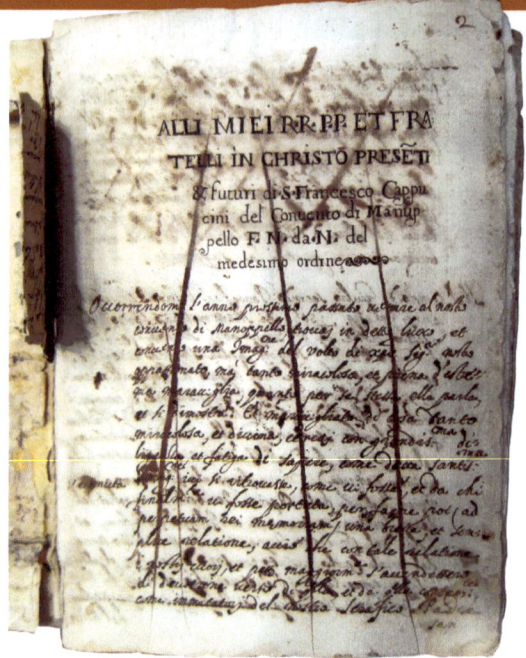

in the archives of the convent of San Michele in L'Aquila, mentioned in Tussio.[153] Although written in an orderly, regular hand, it looks like a service copy; the final part and the name of the author are missing.[154] The fourth manuscript, kept in Manoppello, has a different title from those conserved in L'Aquila,[155] and the text also diverges from the others in several parts. It presents a stage in the drawing up of the *Relatione,* prior to its final state, and pre-dates the other documents[156] [fig. 75]. It can be defined as a draft of the *Relatione*, containing rewritings, sometimes contained in small scrolls of paper glued onto the document, and corrections. Some of the latter rectify mistakes that had been made in the copying of a preceding text,[157] and others seem to be variants made by the author, which suggests that the author of the manuscript is da Bomba. The Manoppello manuscript is "signed" with the initials "N. from N." Lastly, there is a copy of the *Relatione* from the 1800s, where several glosses have been added in the margin. This was carried out by the Capuchin friar Eugenio da Manoppello, and is kept in the provincial archives of the Capuchin friars in L'Aquila.[158]

Fig. 76. The *Holy Face* of Manoppello compared with the *Face of Christ* by Fra Angelico, c. 1446-1447, fragment of detached fresco; Rome, National Museum of Palazzo Venezia.

The Unmistakable Features of Christ

How could Heinrich Pfeiffer formulate this hypothesis?

Unlike the burial cloths of the Shroud of Turin and the Shroud of Oviedo,[159] the Holy Face (17.5 x 24 cm, visible on both sides) is a veil so thin as to be transparent; it is possible to read a book through it. As it is the only portrait on a veil that has come down to us,[160] it is difficult to explain how it was painted/imprinted on both sides, retaining the transparency of the threads. The image appears to be one with the fabric, and to be composed of variations of gray-brown, with the lips and wounds on the sides of the face more rose-colored. Exposed to sunlight, the image becomes a warm yellow, almost golden. This rare phenomenon is one of the reasons that have led to the hypothesis that the veil could be of marine byssus (an ancient and precious textile fiber, common in the area of the Mediterranean, obtained from the filaments of some mollusks).[161]

On the face of Manoppello, we find all the characteristic features of Christ summarized by Nicephorus Callistus Xanthopoulos:

Fig. 75 (*facing*). Donato da Bomba, draft of the *Relatione historica* kept in Manoppello and probably signed by him.

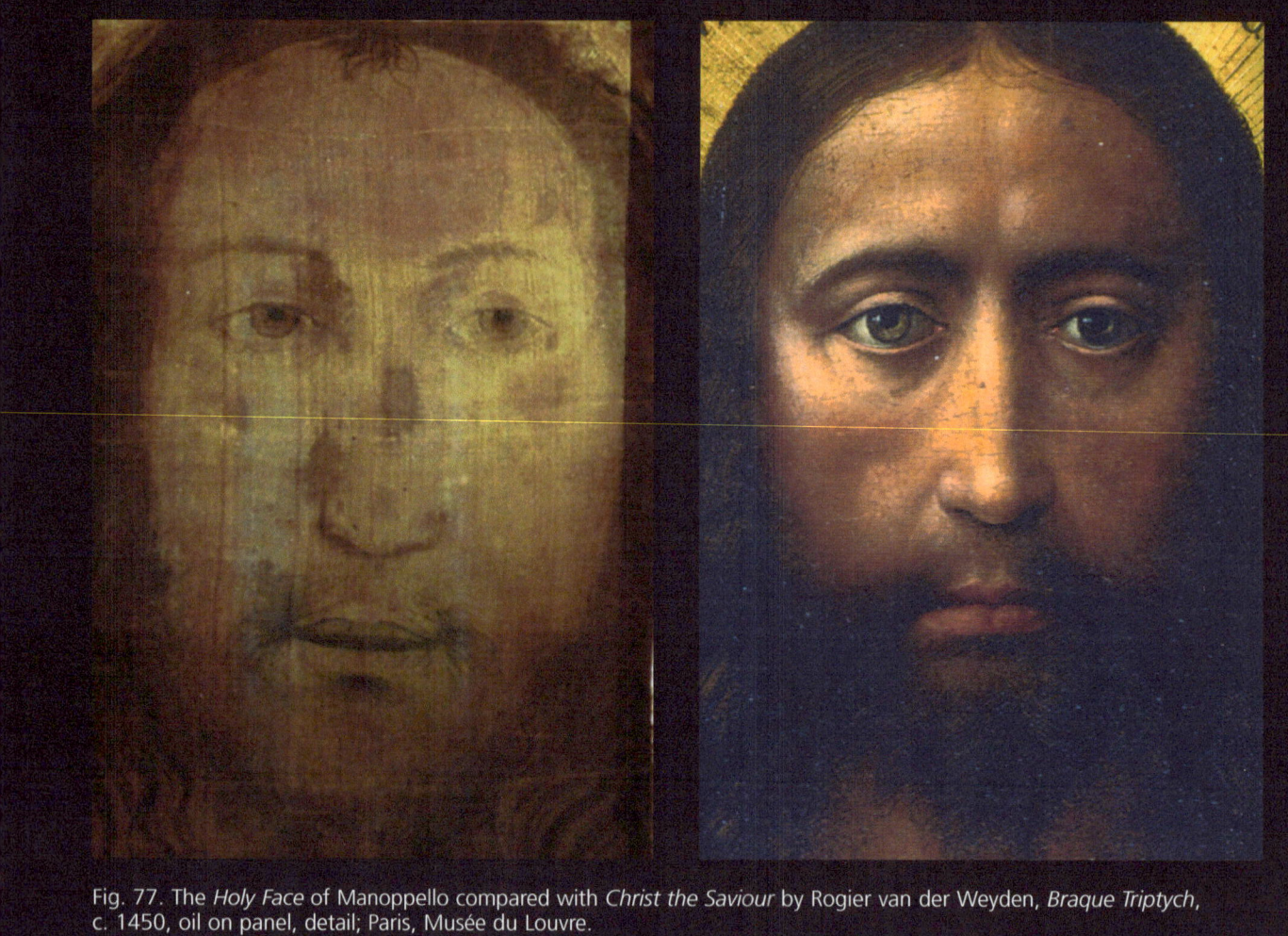

Fig. 77. The *Holy Face* of Manoppello compared with *Christ the Saviour* by Rogier van der Weyden, *Braque Triptych*, c. 1450, oil on panel, detail; Paris, Musée du Louvre.

"He had fair hair, not too thick but slightly curly at the ends; black eyebrows not entirely arched; brown vivacious eyes full of inexpressible charm, a long nose, the hair of his beard reddish and short, he wore his hair long, and it was never cut by scissors or touched by human hands except those of his Mother when he was still a child. The head was slightly tilted forward, and this somewhat reduced his height. The color of his skin was similar to that of wheat. The face was neither round nor oval, and especially in the lower part, looked very like that of his Mother. Seriousness, prudence, unalterable gentleness and clemency breathed from his person. Finally, in all respects, he resembled his divine and virgin Mother."[162]

We find a strong connection with the Face of Manoppello not only in many reproductions of the Roman Veronica (above all in the German, French and Flemish works of the fourteenth and fifteenth centuries), but also in depictions of Christ. There is a notable similarity, for example, with the *Face of Christ* [fig. 76][163] in the fragment of the fresco by Fra Angelico, who arrived in Rome in 1445 at the invitation of Pope

Fig. 78. The *Holy Face* of Manoppello compared with the *Holy Mandylion*, detail; Genoa, Church of St Bartholomew of the Armenians.

Eugene IV. The shadows around the eye sockets correspond, as do the lips, the beard, the gaze, the curvature of the eyebrows, the moustache and their attachment to the lips, and the full face. Another example is that of the Flemish Rogier van der Weyden who painted *Christ the Savior* [fig. 77] after his pilgrimage to Rome for the Jubilee in 1450. The paintings of Van der Weyden became a model for all Flemish painters, and for Antonello da Messina. In addition to these various close similarities, the veil of Manoppello also displays many of the characteristic features of the *acheiropoieton* images of Christ, in particular those attributed to the Roman Veronica.

Superimposition with the Face of the Shroud

In the studies of Sr Blandina Paschalis Schlömer, there is support for the closest relationship between the image of the veil of Manoppello and the face imprinted on the Shroud of Turin. This relationship is so close as to allow the total overlapping of the Holy Face with the face on the Shroud. In addition to this, there is

Fig. 79. The *Holy Face* of Manoppello compared with the *Mandylion* of Laon (cf. fig. 44).

also full compatibility with the bloodstains on the *Sudarium* of Oviedo. The Holy Face shows the same wounds – the deformed left cheek, the swollen and bloody lips – which have been detected on the Shroud.

The *Kamouliana*

The *Kamouliana*, the oldest *acheiropoieton* image of Christ, has been described as an object that gave the impression of being neither painted nor woven. Fr Heinrich Pfeiffer observes that "until now no object has been found which, after a brief examination of its surface, gives us exactly the same impression – that it was neither painted nor woven – other than the Holy Face of Manoppello."[164]

In 1998-1999, Donato Vittore, a professor in the Faculty of Medicine at Bari University in Italy, investigated the veil using a high resolution digital scanner. His results declared that no paint residue could be seen in the space between the warp thread and that of the weft.[165] Other investigations in microscopy and spectroscopy have been carried out by Giulio Fanti, professor of mechanical engineering and thermal energy at the University of Padova, Italy.[166] Ultraviolet light analyses carried out

Fig. 80. The *Holy Face* of Manoppello compared with the *Holy Keramion*, 12th century, Russian icon by the Novgorod School; Moscow, Tretjakow Gallery.

with a Wood's lamp have confirmed a test that had already been carried out in 1971 – neither the fabric nor the image of the Face show appreciable fluorescence, as would be expected in the presence of substances of the amalgam of colors, while a strong fluorescence appears where there are evident signs of restoration in the top left and right corners. The analysis in infrared light also showed the absence of a preparatory sketch underneath the image and the absence of corrections. Significant traces of substances (pigments? dirt? glue?) seem to be present on other limited parts of the veil.

The *Mandylion* and the *Keramion*

The differences between the *Mandylion* (the cloth) and the *Keramion* (the tile) are seen first and foremost in their backgrounds. The fringes indicate the towel of the *Mandylion* and the yellow ocher the clay of the *Keramion*. In the face of Christ the differences between the two icons are in the direction of the gaze and of the small tuft of hair falling over his forehead, and they seem to emphasize the fact that one is a copy reflecting the other – in the *Mandylion* the gaze and hair is turned towards the right and in the *Keramion* both are turned towards the left

Fig. 81. *Veronica's Veil*, c. 1425, fresco in the choir; Frankfurt am Main, Cathedral.

[figs. 79-80]. Interestingly, due to its unique feature of being equally visible on the two faces of the veil, the Holy Face of Manoppello contains within itself both the *Mandylion* and the *Keramion*. Since it is impossible to define which is the "principal side" of the veil of Abruzzo, it is plausible that copies made from one side or the other are the source of legends of the reflected copy imprinted on the stone in the recess of the wall.

Furthermore, when the veil is placed against a black background it is remarkably similar – especially in the slant of the eyes – to the Byzantine copy of the *Mandylion* preserved in Genoa [fig. 78]. The ancient icon was donated by Emperor John V Palaeologus to Leonardo Montaldo.

The Transparency of the Veil

Regarding the transparency mentioned by Luther ("It is simply a black square tablet, upon which hangs a transparent fabric"), some artists, especially in the Flemish region, show the veil of Veronica as transparent. Since 1400, the effect of transparency was a characteristic of the depiction of precious veils, such as the mantles of the Madonna and of the Child Jesus. Comparison of such art with the veil in Manoppello, however, which actually is semi-transparent, is quite extraordinary.

Fig. 82. Transparency of the Manoppello veil exposed to light.

The visibility of the image on both sides of the veil does not seem to be a consequence of the transparency of the fabric, because the intensity of the colors is identical on both sides, and the two images do not seem to be perfect mirror images.[167]

The Visible Teeth

The face of Christ in the mosaic in the apse of Santa Maria in Trastevere [fig. 86] in Rome (1290) closely resembles the *Mandylion* of Laon [fig. 44]. However, the artist represented Christ's half-open mouth with visible teeth. These characteristics, open eyes and visible teeth, are also found on an altarpiece painted by an anonymous Polish artist for a convent in Warsaw in 1350 [fig. 87]. Given the difficulty it takes an artist to represent a half-open mouth with visible teeth (which is also found on an ivory *osculum pacis*, in which the face on the veil is 25 mm high [fig. 85]), it follows that the prototype which the artists referred to must have been an authoritative one. Without doubt, visible teeth are not a characteristic deriving from copies of the *Mandylion* or the Shroud; it can thus be considered a characteristic of the Veronica, as reported in Piazza's *Emerologio*.[168] The veil of Manoppello also presents this characteristic [fig. 82].

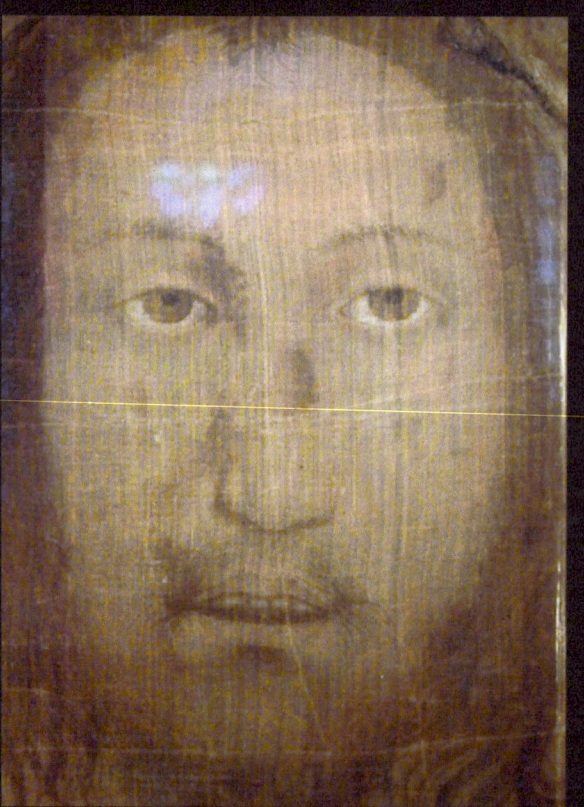 

Fig. 83. The *Holy Face* of Manoppello with the teeth showing.

Fig. 84. Pietro Cavallini, *Christ*, detail of the *Last Judgement*, c. 1293, fresco; Rome, Basilica of St Cecilia in Trastevere.

Fig. 85. *The Holy Face Carried by an Angel*, c. 1470, ivory pax, detail; Paderborn, Westphalia, Archbishop's Diocesan Museum.

Fig. 86. *Jesus Enthroned*, 12th century, mosaic, detail; Rome, Basilica of St Mary in Trastevere.

Fig. 87. *The Holy Face Venerated by St Francis and St Clare*, c. 1350, tempera and gold leaf on wood, devotional panel, detail; Warsaw, National Museum (from the Poor Clares' Monastery in Breslau).

Fig. 88. The *Holy Face* of Manoppello compared with *Christ Crowned with Thorns* by Hans Memling, c. 1480, oil on panel; Genoa, Palazzo Bianco, Gallery.

Signs of Suffering

In *Christ Crowned with Thorns* by Hans Memling [fig. 88] and in the Holy Face, the bruise on the left cheekbone caused by "the blow of Malchus"[169] is evident.

The sparse beard of the Abruzzo image is torn, as prophesied by Isaiah. The affinity is striking between the veil of Manoppello and Bosch's *Christ Mocked* at the National Gallery in London, where the henchman at the right is caught in the act of tearing his beard [fig. 89]. The similarity in these faces is such that, if it were established that the Manoppello veil is a work of art, its author should be sought among the Flemish.

Final Questions

For historical research, the question remains as to whether the hypothesis suggested by Father Heinrich Pfeiffer – that the veil of Manoppello is to be identified with the Roman Veronica – is true or not. Is there any other object equally perfect and corresponding to the fourteenth

Fig. 89. The *Holy Face* of Manoppello compared with *Christ Mocked* by Hieronymus Bosch, c. 1485, oil on panel; London, National Gallery.

century hymn *Salve Sancta Facies*? But this is not the only question open. Scientific studies on the veil of Manoppello, begun in the final years of the last century, are made particularly complex by having to be conducted – at present – without removing the image from the seventeenth century crystal glass to avoid the alteration of the state of equilibrium of the tissue and its consequent deterioration. From these studies, made only with the aid of non-invasive optical instruments, we await data regarding the formation of the image on the veil, the nature of the fabric (in 2007, the hypothesis was advanced that it could be made from marine byssus[170]) and the relationship between the Holy Face and the Shroud of Turin.[171]

Further tests will certainly help provide new insights but, as has been the case for the Shroud, it is difficult to arrive at a declaration of the nature of the *acheiropoieton* images. The question of the origin of the veil will, in all probability, remain open. Even if it could be established that the veil of Manoppello is not made by human hands, the question which Emperor Constantine VII asked, as soon as he came into contact with the face of Jesus, will remain: Is it the reward for the compassionate gesture of a woman on the steep road to Calvary, or is it the face cloth that Peter and John saw in the tomb on Easter morning? The mysterious origin of the Holy Face was evoked by the Orthodox theologian Olivier Clément in the Way of the Cross at the Colosseum in 1998: "Your Holy Face, which was imprinted on the veil of Veronica, the one received from a king of Edessa, or that of the Shroud burned by the fire of the Spirit, is replicated and multiplied in our churches to teach us to discover, under many guises, the face of man, and under many masks, the face of God."[172]

The purpose of our study was to learn about the history of the depictions of Christ and understand what the gift of His image that He Himself left the Church means for us. Many answers are spread throughout the centuries, among which the one offered by St Bridget stands out: "This sweat flowed from my face for the solace of future generations."[173]

Fig. 90. The *Holy Face* of Manoppello. The open door of the shrine at the end of the nave is visible through the veil.

"WHOEVER CONTEMPLATES ME, CONSOLES ME"

I want my Face, which reflects the pains in my soul, the sorrow and love of my heart, to be honored more. Whoever contemplates me consoles me. [Pierina De Micheli, First Friday of Lent, 1936.][174]

Donato da Bomba

Description of the Most Holy Image

He has a rather long, well-proportioned face, with a venerable and majestic look, which at the same time somehow induces both terror and love in the onlooker. Part of him corrects you, the other part allures you; part of him provokes penitence, the other part compassion. The terror induces great, humble reverence, the love great and steadfast trust. Hence those who gaze on it are never satiated with contemplating it, and wish to always have it before their eyes. And when they eventually leave it, with heavy sighs full of love, they are forced to leave him their hearts, bathed in tears.

His hair, or we could say locks, are long, with thin, twisted curls in typical Nazarene style, of a color that tends towards black; and every single hair in that great head of hair can be distinguished one from another, and in particular at the top of the forehead about fifty hairs wind into a little corkscrew, distinct from each other and well arranged, which looks such a marvel that onlookers wonder whether it is something divine or human.

His left cheek is swollen and bigger than the other because of the strong blow across his cheek that was given to him in the presence of the high priest Caiphas, according to the Evangelists. Which does not surprise me greatly, seeing that our father St Bernard, in a certain sermon that he wrote about the Passion of the Lord, affirms that that sacrilegious man's hand was armed with a metal glove when he hit our Lord across the cheek, as was usual in those times and still is equally usual in our times. St Vincent Ferrer adds that on receiving such a hard blow across his cheek Christ fell to the ground, both due to the suddenness of the gesture and also finding Himself in such pain and weakened because of the many wounds, blows and other ill treatment that he had received in the garden, when the Jews took Him. He had lost a lot of blood because of this, and lastly, because of such a hard blow, He was spitting blood from his mouth.

The lips are very swollen, raised on both the upper and the lower lip, more the upper one than the lower because of the many punches He received on that bitter, sorrowful night of His passion; His teeth show, more the upper teeth than the lower ones, and they move those who look on Him to tremendous compassion.

His beard is the same color as the hair on His head, not very long, but thin and torn for the same reasons, I mean because of the ill-treatment he received, which, if told, together with the revelations made to St Bridget, St Elizabeth, Miltiades and other saints, as well as those told by the Evangelists, cause so much anxiety.

It seems that the most holy face is made of living flesh, but flesh that is emaciated, sad, afflicted, sorrowful, pale and covered in bruises around the eyes and on the forehead, that

Fig. 91 (facing). *The Holy Face*, Manoppello, Pescara, Shrine of the Holy Face.

rightly it can be said that it is a living yet silent script, because in the Greek language, the noun "painting" also means "script" [writing], where we can read of all the extreme, harsh pains that our Savior suffered for love of us during his mostly holy passion. Jesus Christ our Savior suffered extreme sorrow when He was beaten, wounded, whipped, crowned with thorns and in a hard, worse than harsh, death nailed to the cross; but in the face He always showed, even in the images and paintings miraculously made of him, all His painful and bitter sorrows, so that in a vivid way, reading it and contemplating it might stimulate us, with our great shame and pain together, to be grateful to Him for such a great benefit.

Our most holy image is said to be thus (except in the eyes and the forehead) because the eyes are moderately large, dark and very cheerful; the forehead very spacious and serene, above which a few small wounds can be seen, one bigger than the others, without diminishing the cheerfulness of the eyes and the serenity of the brow. None of that makes me wonder, because since they are the eyes of Christ, as it is written in the Canticle, they are similar to those of a dove, which has no gall, which is the seat of anger, disdain and trouble. For this reason they never felt wrath at anyone. The eyes of Christ cried many times over the wretchedness of sinners, but since they were without the bile of anger, they never raged over sinners; on the contrary, while on the cross, He prayed for those who were crucifying Him and cursing Him. With His loving gaze, He converted St Peter, who had denied him three times, shortly before the good robber, who had cursed Him with His companion on the cross.

The prophet David looked at these eyes, full of compassion and without a trace of anger, when he desired that God look on him with such eyes, so that He would have mercy on him. The holy prophet could not desire a better thing, said our father St Ambrose, because it was impossible for Christ our Savior to look at our wretchedness without feeling compassion; being without the poison of anger or disdain, his eyes are always cheerful, full of mercy, benign and compassionate towards everyone.

We can also say the same about His divine, regal forehead, which must have always been crowned with serene cheerfulness, and no sadness ever appeared on it. Because although, as the philosophers say, the forehead is the seat of shame, so that when one is ashamed of something disgraceful, that has not been well done or said, the forehead always betrays it, as happened to our forebears in the earthly Paradise, who had sinned, having found out that they were naked, and deprived of many graces and favors because of the shame they felt, they fled, and hid from God's face; nonetheless, since Christ by nature was foreign to all sin, having been blessed and glorious from the first moment of His conception, He could not because of this be ashamed of those things which He voluntarily suffered, so as to be able to free man from His own shame. On the contrary, being unable to be ashamed, He considered what He suffered all glory and honor, the very substance of His empire, principality and crown. Hence it follows that leaving an imprint of His living portrait on our sacred picture, although it was

Fig. 92 (*facing*). Ridolfo Ghirlandaio, *Ascent to Calvary*, c. 1505 oil on canvas, detail; London, National Gallery.

Fig. 93. *Veronica with Veil,* 1550, monumental calvary, Guéhenno in Morbihan, Brittany.

after His passion, and thus sad, afflicted, pale, bruised, sorrowful, on the forehead, however, He is serene and tranquil, and with most cheerful eyes, which sparks off rays of grace, lights of glory and splendid piety in the hearts and minds of those who look at Him with devotion.

[(Donato da Bomba O.F.M. Cap.), *Relatione historica d'una miracolosa imagine del volto di Christo signor nostro passionato*, L'Aquila, Archivio provinciale F.M. Cap., 48r-51r]

Karol Wojtyła

The Name

In the crowd walking towards the place
                    [of the Agony – did you
open up a gap at some point or were you
                        [opening it
from the beginning?
And since when? You tell me, Veronica.
Your name was born in the very instant
in which your heart
became an effigy: the effigy of truth.
Your name was born from what you gazed upon.

[Karol Wojtyła, "Il nome", from *La redenzione cerca la tua forma per entrare nell'inquietudine di ogni uomo*, in Id., *Tutte le poesie*, Corriere della Sera, Milano 2005, pp. 63-68]

Luigi Giussani

"Your name was born from what you gazed upon" (Karol Wojtyla)
The law of existence is love: to affirm with one's own actions something other than myself. All of life is in function of something greater, it's in function of God; our life is in function of You, O Christ: "I seek your face." "I seek your face", this is the essence of time. "I seek your face", this is the essence of the heart. "I seek your face", this is the nature of reason.

[Luigi Giussani, *Egli solo è*, San Paolo, Milano 2005, pp. 20-21]

Paolo Martinelli

Where does the widespread interest in the Holy Face and portraits of Christ running through the history of the Church come from? Why was it even necessary to have a council in Nicaea in 787 to decide on the legitimacy of venerating such images? What is at stake, even today, is the reality of the incarnation and its significance for us as human beings. The relationship that God desired to have with us is not entrusted to our religious imagination. He really "became flesh" (Jn 1:14). God did not unite Himself generically to humanity. The mystery became One among us.

This is why the very person of Jesus Christ, his actions, words and face are something unique and real. God communicated Himself to us in a unique form, distinguishable from all others. His beauty is unique, his splendor transcends all measure.

Benedict XVI affirmed that "this beauty is not simply a harmony of forms: 'the most handsome of men'(Ps 45:3) is also He who 'has no majestic bearing to draw our eye nor beauty to draw us to Him' (Is 55:2). Jesus Christ can transfigure 'even the dark mystery of death into the radiant light of the resurrection' (*Sacramentum caritatis*, n. 35)."

In this regard, Don Julián Carrón (President of the Fraternity of Communion and Liberation), quoting Msg. Luigi Giussani, reminds us that "if Christ's name 'did not have a personality that at a certain point becomes autonomous, if He did not have an ultimately unique face, with unmistakable features that cannot be confused even with those that He created as a sign of Himself,' Christ would lose that 'ultimate, unmistakable uniqueness. If Christ were to lose that ultimate uniqueness, [...] the rest is not enough" (*Exercises of the Fraternity*, Rimini 2008, p. 30). Our faith rests on this unique and unmistakable figure of Christ.

A people, the Church, is what corresponds now to this incomparable face – the generation that "seeks your face" (cf. Ps. 24:6). It is precisely this search that makes the people of the Church, in turn, unique in history, a people composed of peoples. This original relationship between Christ and the Church, between His face and His people, is well documented in the way the images of Christ throughout history are linked to the presence of the numerous faithful who have been drawn together by them. The face of Christ – as this volume shows – is inextricably linked to the human lives of those who belong to Him, to "those He has created as a sign of Himself" (L. Giussani, *L'attrattiva Gesù*, Bur, Milano 1999, p. 148).

This testifies to the fact that our access to the person of Christ is never solitary, but comes about in community. The people of God recognize their own identity while searching for His face. We find His face by belonging to His people. The uniqueness of His face is thus mirrored in human reality, in men and women who belong to Him and bear witness to Him in front of the whole world.

Why, then, do we seek His face? And why do we not stop seeking it, once we have found it? What is the attraction that His unmistakable features hold for the hearts of men and women? Karol Wojtyla answers this question in an evocative way in his poem on Veronica: "Your name was born from what you gazed upon."

The mystery of an encounter from which

Fig. 94. Georges Rouault, *Christ Carries the Cross Below Veronica's Veil*, 1934-1936, woodcut from the *Passion of Christ cycle*; private collection.

our name springs is contained in this image. In Holy Scripture, names indicate the very nature of a person, the uniqueness in each person. In the poem by Blessed John Paul II, the name springs from the encounter with the face of Christ. Gazing at that face, one finds oneself. This is why Veronica is emblematic of the drama of each one of us, in every age.

It is in the search for Christ's face that our deepest desire is made manifest. Indeed, whether we know it or not, each person seeks that gaze to recognize his or her own true self. Finding that face, and rediscovering His presence in people today is therefore the fundamental answer to human desire. Encountering Christ dissolves our enigmatic condition and allows us to live according to the stature of our desire.

[Foreword of *Il Volto ritrovato. I tratti inconfondibili di Cristo*, Edizioni di Pagina, Bari 2013, pp. 7-8]

Angelo Scola

"I live like a man chased out of his own personality and condemned at the same time to investigate it to the depths." This was how, from the first line placed on the lips of his Adam, one of the protagonists of *Rays of Paternity*, Karol Wojtyla identified this constitutive drama in the heart of each man. Each one of us perceives him or herself as being far from oneself, "chased out of their personality" and contemporaneously near oneself (condemned to investigate it to the depths). And yet, no matter how far we may be alienated from our own hearts – from the center of our I – we must always come to terms with the "question of all questions" which, like wild grass in Spring, pokes up from under even the thickest pile of rubbish. It is ingeniously expressed by Leopardi in his poem about the wandering shepherd in Asia: "And who am I?"

What does this question seek? It is chasing, with laboured breath, that peace in which our restless heart can at last find rest.

Now there were some Greeks among those who had come up to worship at the feast. They came to Philip, who was from Bethsaida in Gal-

ilee, and asked him, "Sir, we wish to see Jesus." Philip went and told Andrew; then Andrew and Philip went and told Jesus (cf. Jn 12:20-22).

The desire of those Greeks sets off a kind of "chain reaction" of communication: from Philip to Andrew, from these two together, to Jesus. The very fabric of relations between men and women is, in a certain sense, placed in motion by the desire to see Jesus, to see the face of God. "My soul thirsts for God, the living God. When can I enter and see the face of God?" (Ps. 42: 3).

How can this desire be realized? What is the path to recognising and seeing Jesus? "In order to see Jesus, we have to let ourselves be looked at by him",[175] John Paul II answered us in decisive, unequivocal fashion, commenting on the passage from John. And, in this way, it introduces us to the overturning of the method that Christian faith brought into this world: no longer our search for the face of God, but His gaze on our face!

Letting ourselves be looked at by Christ: this is the path that our thirsty hearts must follow in order to be quenched, so that the desire at the

Fig. 95 (*facing*). Master of the Bamberg Altar, *Veronica's Veil*, c. 1430, detail of Walburg's epitaph (from the Church of Our Lady of Nuremberg); Nuremberg, Germanisches Nationalmuseum.

depths of our being may be fulfilled. And thus, in the Face of Jesus looking at us, our face takes form. Every man and every woman, indeed, takes form from the gaze of that Man, who calls our freedom – this is vocation – to be involved with him.

[From the speech by cardinal Angelo Scola, *"Tu mi guardi dalla croce"*, *Cristo destino dell'uomo* (You look at me from the cross, Christ, Man's Destiny), Belluno, April 3, 2004]

Bruno Forte

How does man perceive God in history according to the Old and New Testaments? There are two principal ways, witnessed to in both Testaments: listening and seeing. To say that the world of the Bible is only one of listening – given the objective importance of the invitation to listen contained, for example, in the formula *Shema Israel Adonai Elohenu Adonai Echad* "listen, Israel, the Lord is our God, the Lord alone" (Deut. 6:4) – is in fact a reduction. In the world of the Bible, listening is of fundamental importance because the Word is central; nonetheless, in both the Old and New Testaments, listening is inseparable from seeing. In the Old Testament's prophetic books, it is common to find forms of the verb 'to see' used with terms associated with 'listening' (in Ezechiel and Isaiah, for example). The culmination of this can be found in the book of Revelation, 1:12: in a grandiose scene, the seer is on the island of Patmos on the day of the Lord, in a liturgical context, and hears a sound like falling water. He turns round to "see the voice", as the Greek text says literally, *blèpein ten phonèn*. *Blèpein* is the verb used in Greek to mean "to look insistently and hard", to scrutinize, or look intensely. In the expression in Revelation 1:12, the object of this intense, persevering, penetrating gaze is the voice, *ten phonèn*. There is a continuous need for a vision which can be linked to listening. Keeping in mind that the Hebrew word *panim* (face) is a plural term which can also mean *dual*, one understands that, as in listening, also seeing God's face (in a certain sense) will never come to an end.

If the Face is in fact Faces, then God too offers Himself as an endless sea of Faces to scrutinize. The plural *panim* tells us that our search for the Face will be continuous, therefore the way to perceive the divine in time will be a continual listening to the word in order to see the Face ever more deeply, up to the point of what theological tradition calls "seeing God in his eternal face."

It is therefore legitimate for the believer not only to listen to the Word of God, but to simultaneously try to see the Face of God. What is the answer to this legitimate aspiration given by God in the Bible? In other words, what is the structure of divine self-communication in history? According to the Second Nicene Council and the Fourth Council of Constantinople, which put an end to the iconoclastic crisis (that is the negation of the possibility and legitimacy of holy images), there are two ways in which God satisfies this aspiration to hear the voice by seeing the voice. According to the formula of the Fourth Council of Constantinople, they are the *lògos en syllabè*, speech in syllables, and *graphè en kromàsi*, writing in color, in light. Hence, there are two languages of the sacred: a verbal language and a visual language. By the faith of the Church, this is founded on the fact that life made itself visible (1 Jn 1:2), that the Word became flesh (Jn 1:14). If the Word was made flesh, we can be authorized not only to hear His Word, but also in some way to see His Face.

This means that God always reveals Himself in a circumscribed form, whether in a word circumscribed by a sound, or in the graphic form of an image, an icon, which, not coincidentally, is said to be 'written' rather than 'painted' (hence iconography). Along this double road, we are authorized to seek, in a circumscribed form, God's way of speaking of Himself to us in words and images. This is why it is plausible that as once and for all the Word spoke of itself in men's words and revealed itself in the flesh of a historical face, so may He reveal Himself to men not only verbally, but in sacramental form, and even out of absolute gratuitousness, by means of an intervention which shows itself in visible form. Here I am not referring to subjective visions, which is extremely complex from a theological and spiritual point of view, requiring rigorous discernment, but I am saying that what I have said so far justifies why, in Christian tradition, there has always been a great desire for images not painted by human hands. This desire, in other words, is not illegitimate in Christian tradition, because it is God who gave it foundation, given that He made Himself visible and became man. The conclusion to this part is rather modest, but of extreme importance, because if we were to affirm from a theological point of view that no *acheiropoieton* image may exist, we would have to exclude, through prejudice, an investigation in this field. The conclusion we have reached, on the contrary, is that if God is happy to show Himself *in figuris*, both verbally and to our sight, we cannot exclude that He may have left imprints of His visible manifestation, deriving from His being present in history. Naturally, the closer these imprints are to the source, the more eloquent they are. This is why no image will ever render satisfactorily the force of meeting the Word in the flesh as much as the holy places, where Jesus walked. I'm thinking of Peter's house in Capernaum, or of the way along the west wall of the Temple, precious places because of the imprint of a Presence that has been there.

Secondly, what interpretation can we give of the image, and in particular of an image not painted by human hands? If God speaks of Himself in words and shows Himself in a colored image, then the image must be read as the *logos* must be interpreted. This is part of the Judaeo-Christian tradition. Judaism and Christianity are interpretative religions, as Islam is not, since it denies interpretation on principle. Hermeneutics, that is, the science of interpreting, is born within the Jewish-Christian biblical and theological tradition, because God told of Himself, but did not clarify totally what He said about Himself. By means of what He said about Himself, and made us see about Him, we have to go constantly beyond what He said, digging down and plumbing the depths.

I will try to read the image of Manoppello from a theological point of view, treating some elements as possible, while not affirming them in some absolute way, because we are not in a

Fig. 96. Anonymous Burgundian artist, *Veronica with the Veil*, mid-14th century, stone with traces of color; Dijion, Musée des Beaux-Arts.

field where mathematical certainty has to be affirmed; rather, moral certainty is enough. What does the depiction of this Face tell us? I think it tells us three fundamental facts. The first is a strong underlining of the historical subject of our faith. We do not believe in a myth, we believe in a historical revelation which passed through a man who we recognize to be the Son of God, who was visible, touchable, and who was touched, seen, heard, and who uttered words. This appears very strongly in this Holy Face, a very human face that underlines that the subject of the revelation was the Son of God, Jesus. The second aspect is that this Jesus reveals Himself in this Face with the two fundamental aspects of *passus* and *glorificatus*. It is a face which carries within it the marks of the Passion, but at the same time, it is a face which radiates luminosity, the victory of Light over darkness. While recalling to us the historical nature of the passion, it also reminds us of the historical authenticity of the original witness about victory over death. In the Face of Manoppello, the risen aspect is more visible than in the Shroud of Turin. In that shroud, one has more the idea of *Christus Passus*. At Manoppello, you can perceive the paradoxical unity of *passus* and *glorificatus*, which is a theme that runs throughout all Christian iconography, in which the risen Christ is often portrayed with the wounds of the passion. Therefore, we are faced with the paradoxical union of death and resurrection. The third indication that the image gives us is that not only *passus* and *glorificatus* are represented, but also *patiens* and *glorificans*. That is, He who we see in this image is He whom is in a certain sense suffering, but is

Fig. 97. Jan van Eyck, *Polyptych of the Mystical Lamb*, 1426-1432, oil on panel, detail; Ghent, Cathedral of St Bavo.

also winning over pain, and is communicating victory over sorrow and death: the participles are not only in the past, but also in the present.

The experience of interpreting this image does not only belong to *that time*, but is also *today and forever*. It is as though both the act of the Passion and of the Resurrection are fixed in eternity. On the other hand, in the Book of Revelation, the Lamb sacrificed while standing says exactly the same things: the most precious biblical source for this is not only John 20:7 (Peter arrives and sees the Veil and the *sudarium*...) but also Revelation, with the image of the sacrificed lamb, of *Christus Passus et Glorificatus* who is at the same time *Patiens et Glorificans*.

[From the speech given by the Archbishop of Chieti-Vasto, Monsignor Bruno Forte, *Il Volto Santo di Manoppello e la plausibilità teologica delle immagini acheropite*, 25 January 2007][176]

Benedict XVI

During my pause for prayer just now, I was thinking of the first two Apostles who, urged by John the Baptist, followed Jesus to the banks of the River Jordan, as we read at the beginning of John's Gospel (cf. 1:35-37). The Evangelist recounts that Jesus turned around and asked them: "What do you seek?" And they answered him, "Rabbi... where are you staying?" And he said to them, "Come and see" (cf. Jn 1:38-39). That very same day, the two who were following Him had an unforgettable experience which prompted them to say: "We have found the Messiah" (Jn 1:41). The One whom a few hours earlier they had thought of as a simple "rabbi" had acquired a very precise identity – the identity of Christ who had been awaited for centuries. But, in fact, what a long journey still lay ahead of those disciples! They could not even imagine how profound the mystery of Jesus of Nazareth could be or how unfathomable, inscrutable, His "Face" would prove, so that even after living with Jesus for three years, Philip, who was one of them, was to hear Him say at the Last Supper: "Have I been with you so long, and yet you do not know me, Philip?" And then the words that sum up the novelty of Jesus' revelation: "He who has seen me has seen the Father" (Jn 14:9). Only after His Passion when they encountered Him Risen, when the Spirit enlightened their minds and their hearts, would the Apostles understand the significance of the words Jesus had spoken and recognize Him as the Son of God, the Messiah promised for the world's redemption. They were then to become His unflagging messengers, courageous witnesses even to martyrdom.

Fig. 98. Pope Benedict XVI praying in Manoppello before the Holy Face.

"He who has seen me has seen the Father." Yes, dear brothers and sisters, to "see God" it is necessary to know Christ and to let oneself be molded by His Spirit who guides believers "into all the truth" (cf. Jn 16:13). Those who meet Jesus, who let themselves be attracted by Him and are prepared to follow Him even to the point of sacrificing their lives, personally experience, as He did on the Cross, that only the "grain of wheat" that falls to the earth and dies, bears "much fruit" (cfr. Jn 12:24). This is the path of Christ, the way of total love that overcomes death. He who takes it and "hates his life in this world will keep it for eternal life" (Jn 12:25). In other words, he lives in God already on this earth, attracted and transformed by the dazzling brightness of His Face. This is the experience of God's true friends, the saints who, in the brethren, especially the poorest and neediest, recognized and loved the Face of that God, lovingly contemplated for hours in prayer. For us they are encouraging examples to imitate; they assure us that if we follow this path, the way of love, with fidelity, we too, as the Psalmist sings, will be satisfied with God's presence (cf. Ps 17[16]:15).

"Jesu [...] quam bonus te quaerentibus! – How kind you are, Jesus, to those who seek you!" This is what we have just sung in the *dulcis memoria*" [*Jesus, the very thought of you*], which some people attribute to St Bernard. It is a hymn that acquires rare eloquence in the Shrine dedicated to the Holy Face, which calls to mind Psalm 24[23]: "Such is the generation of those who seek him, who seek the face of the God of Jacob" (v. 6). But which is "the generation" of those who seek the Face of God, which generation deserves to "ascend the hill of the Lord" and "stand in his holy place"? The Psalmist explains: It consists of those who have "clean hands and a pure heart", who do not speak falsehoods, who do not "swear deceitfully" to their neighbor (cf. vv. 3-4). Therefore, in order to enter into communion with Christ and to contemplate His Face, to recognize the Lord's Face in the faces of the brethren and in daily events, we require "clean hands and a pure heart." Clean hands, that is, a life illumined by the truth of love that overcomes indifference, doubt, falsehood and selfishness; and pure hearts are essential too, hearts enraptured by divine beauty, as the Little Thérèse

Fig. 99. Manoppello (Pescara). The Shrine of the Holy Face on the Tarigni hill.

of Lisieux says in her prayer to the Holy Face, hearts stamped with the hallmark of the Face of Christ.

"Your Face, O Lord, I seek": seeking the Face of Jesus must be the longing of all of us Christians; indeed, we are "the generation" which seeks His Face in our day, the Face of the "God of Jacob." If we persevere in our quest for the Face of the Lord, at the end of our earthly pilgrimage, He, Jesus, will be our eternal joy, our reward and glory for ever: "Sis Jesu nostrum gaudium, qui es futurus praemium: sit nostra in te gloria, per cuncta semper saecula."

This is the certainty that motivated the saints of your Region, among whom I would like to mention in particular Gabriel of Our Lady of Sorrows and Camillus de Lellis; our reverent remembrance and our prayer is addressed to them. But let us now address a thought of special devotion to the "Queen of all the Saints", the Virgin Mary, whom you venerate in the various shrines and chapels scattered across the valleys and mountains of the Abruzzi Region. May Our Lady, in whose face – more than in any other creature – we can recognize the features of the Incarnate Word, watch over the families and parishes and over the cities and nations of the whole world.

Dear brothers and sisters, as I thank you once again for your presence and for your gifts, I invoke the Blessing of God upon you and upon all your loved ones with the ancient biblical formula: "May the Lord bless you and keep you: may the Lord make his face to shine upon you and be gracious to you: may the Lord lift up his countenance upon you and give you peace" (cf. Nm 6:24-26). Amen!

[Benedict XVI, Manoppello, September 1, 2006]

Lord Jesus, / As the first apostles, / Whom you asked: "What do you seek?", / Accepted your invitation to: "Come and See" / Recognizing you as the Son of God, / The Promised Messiah for the world's redemption, / We too, your disciples in this difficult time / Want to follow you and be your friends, / Drawn by the brilliance of your face much desired yet hidden.

Show us, we pray you, your face ever new, / That mirror, mystery laden, of God's infinite mercy. / Grant that we may contemplate it / With the eyes of our mind and our hearts: / The Son's face, radiance of the Father's glory / And the imprint of his Nature (cf. Hb 1:3), / The human face of God that has burst into history / To reveal the horizons of eternity. / The silent face of Jesus suffering and risen, / When loved and accepted changes the heart and life. / "Your face, Lord, do I seek, / Do not hide your face from me" (Ps. 27:8 ff).

How many times through the centuries and millenia has not resounded / The ardent invocation of the Psalmist among the faithful! / Lord, with faith, we too repeat the same invocation: / "Man of suffering, as one from whom others

Fig. 100 The *Holy Face* at the centre of the nave in the Manoppello shrine for the procession of the third Sunday in May. The upper corners of the veil show the less transparent repairs made in the 17th century.

hide their faces" (Is. 53:3), / Do not hide your face from us! / We want to draw from your eyes, / That look on us with tenderness and compassion. / The force of love and peace which shows us the way of life, / And the courage to follow you without fear or compromise, / So as to be witnesses of your Gospel, / With concrete signs of acceptance, love and forgiveness.

O Holy Face of Christ, / Light that enlightens the darkness of doubt and sadness, / Life that has defeated forever the force of evil and death, / O inscrutable gaze / That never ceases to watch over men and people, / Face concealed in the Eucharistic signs / And in the faces of those that live with us, / Make us God's pilgrims in this world, / Longing for the Infinite and ready for the final encounter, / When we shall see you, Lord, "face to face" (1Cor. 13: 12), / And be able to contemplate you forever in heavenly Glory / Mary, Mother of the Holy Face, / Help us have "hands innocent and a heart pure", / Hands illumined by the truth of love / And hearts enraptured by divine beauty, / That transformed by the encounter with Christ, / We may gift ourselves to the poor and the suffering, / Whose faces reflect the hidden presence / Of your Son Jesus, / Who lives and reigns forever and ever. Amen!

[September 1, 2007. Prayer sent by Benedict XVI to Mgr. Bruno Forte, Archbishop of Chieti-Vasto, on the first anniversary of the Pope's visit to Manoppello.]

Appendix – Veronica Route (www.veronicaroute.com)

"After this period of distress, during the season when many people go to see the blessed image that Jesus Christ left us as a visible sign of his most beautiful countenance (which my lady beholds in glory), it happened that some pilgrims were going down a street which runs through the center of the city where the most gracious lady was born, lived and died."

[Dante, *Vita Nuova*, XL]

The aim of the Veronica Route online project[177] is to research the nature of the Roman Veronica by ordering its numerous reproductions both geographically and historically.

The project is an attempt to continue the research started by Karl Pearson and published in *Die Fronica* in 1887. Pearson concluded his work thus:

"In our age, in which scholars trace sagas from India to Iceland, I hope my attempt to describe the origin and development of a story which has exercised such a huge influence on the literary and figurative works of our fathers for the last three centuries will not be considered superfluous."[178]

A request for help in completing the project maps was posted on the internet. In response, Veronica images were sent in from as far away as the mediaeval town of Turku in Finland. This led to an unexpected secondary result – the discovery of how great the desire was in Europe to see the Face of Christ.

Fig. 101. *St Veronica with the Veil*, 15th century, stone carving; Nancy, Musée Lorrain.

Fig. 102. The Veronica Route project visualized on Google Earth.

Notes on the Veronica Route website

On each page of the site, there is a copy of the Veronica which has been recorded in the catalog. The images are linked to signposts on the map which are, in turn, linked to a page on the Veronica Route. All the posts are dated and listed chronologically in descending order. Posts which indicate important historical events or periods are enclosed in a blue frame. Those containing texts, such as poems, novels, articles or essays, include the name and photograph of the author.

The Simple Search and Advanced Search functions provide access to the reproduction, period, or place, and enable the user to view them on the pages of both the Veronica Route and Google Earth.

REFERENCES

Sources

Alexandrina Maria da Costa, *Dai diari*.

Alpharani T., *De basilicae Vaticanae antiquissima et nova structura*, Roma 1914.

Ambrogio, *Expositio Evangelii secundum Lucam*.

Anonimo Piacentino, *Itinera Jerosolimitana*.

Benedetto XII, Costituzione *Benedictus Deus*.

Bonifacio VIII, Bolla pontificia *Antiquorum habet fide relatio*.

Borges J.L., *Dreamtigers*, Austin, University of Texas Press, 1964.

Bridget of Sweden, *The Revelations of St Birgitta of Sweden*, New York-Oxford, Oxford University Press, 2006.

Clary R. de, *The Conquest of Constantinople*, translated from the old French by E.H. McNeal, New York, Norton, 1969.

Dante, *Divina Commedia*, transl. by Robert Hollander and Jean Hollander, Princeton Dante Project.

Dante Alighieri, *Vita Nova*, transl. by Mark Musa, Bloomington, Indiana University Press, 1965.

Donato da Bomba, *Relatione historica d'una miracolosa imagine del volto di Christo signor nostro passionato*, L'Aquila, Archivio provinciale FM Cap.

Donato da Bomba OFM Cap., *Vera historia et breve relatione d'una miracolosa imagine del volto di Cristo*, Manoppello, Convento OFM.

Eusebio di Cesarea, *Lettera all'imperatrice Costanza*, in *Textus byzantinos ad iconomachiam pertinentes*, a cura di H. Hennephof, Leiden, Brill, 1969.

Evagrius Scholasticus, *Ecclesiastical History*, translated with an introduction by M. Whitby, Liverpool, Liverpool University Press, 2000.

Frachetto G., *Vitae fratrum ordinis praedicatorum nec cronica ordinis ab anno MCCIII ad MCCCLIV*, in C. Freeman, *Holy bones, holy dust: how relics shaped the history of medieval Europe*, New Haven (CT)-London, Yale University Press, 2012.

Gertrude of Helfta, *Legatus Divinae Pietatis*.

George of Cyprus, *Nouthesia*, ed. Mélioniransky.

George of Pysidia, *De expeditione Heraclii imperatoris contra Persas, libri tres*.

Gregory of Nyssa, *Inventio imaginis in Camulianis*.

Grimaldi G., *Instrumenta autentica translationum ss. Corpum et sacrarum reliquiarum e veteri in novam basilicam*, 1621.

Grimaldi G., *Opusculum de sacrosancto Veronicae Sudario*.

Hackeborn M. von, *Liber specialis gratiae*.

Jacobus de Voragine, *The Golden Legend or Lives of the Saints*, edited by F.S. Ellis, Temple Classics, 1900, www.fordham.edu/halsall/basis/goldenlegend/.

Jerome, *Commentary on Matthew*.

John Paul II, *We wish to see Jesus*, Message on the occasion of the XIX World Youth Day, 22 February 2004.

Julian of Norwich, *Book of Revelations*, www.ccel.org/j/julian/revelations/.

Luther M., *Wider das Papsttum zu Rom, vom Teufel gestiftet*, 1545, WA 54.

Mabillon J., *Museum Italicum*.

Marie de Saint-Pierre, *Vie de la soeur Marie de Saint-Pierre de la Sainte-Famille*, Tours, Oratoire de la Sainte-Face, 1958.

Matthew Paris, *Chronica Majora*.

Merlin and the Grail: Joseph of Arimathea, Merlin, Perceval: the trilogy of prose romances attributed to Robert de Boron, transl. by N. Bryant, Cambridge, D.S. Brewer, 2001.

Monumenta Germaniae Historica, Scriptores, III.

Moroni G., *Dizionario di erudizione storico-ecclesiastica*, Venezia, Tipografia Emiliana, 1861.

Nicephorus Callistus Xanthopulus, *Historia Ecclesiastica*.

Petrarca F., *Il Canzoniere XVI*, transl. by A.S. Kline, 2002, www.poetryintranslation.com.

Piazza C.B., *Emerologio di Roma Cristiana, Ecclesiastica e Gentile*, Tomo I, Roma 1713.

Pientini A., *Le Pie Narrationi delle opere più memorabili fatte in Roma l'anno del giubileo 1575*, traduzione di A. Colaldo, Viterbo 1577.

Sanudo M., *I Diarii*, a cura di R. Fulin, F. Stefani, N. Barozzi, G. Berchet, M. Allegri, Venezia 1879-1903, 58 voll.

Stefaneschi I.G., *De centesimo seu Jubileo anno liber*, trad. M. Cerra, in A. Frugoni, *Pellegrini a Roma nel 1300. Cronache del primo Giubileo*, Casale Monferrato, Piemme, 1999.

Theophylactus Simocattus, *Historiae*.

Textus byzantinos ad iconomachiam pertinentes, a cura di H. Hennephof, Leiden, Brill, 1969.

Torrigio F.M., *Le Sacre Grotte*, Roma 1639², vol. II.

Tussio F. da, *Memorie storiche del Volto Santo*, L'Aquila, Tipografia Vecchioni, 1875.

Valtorta M., *Il Poema dell'Uomo-Dio*, volume IX, Isola del Liri, Centro Editoriale Valtortiano, 1986.

Valtorta M., *L'Evangelo come mi è stato rivelato*, volume X, Isola del Liri, Editrice Pisani, 1975.

Vasari G., *Lives of the most eminent painters, sculptors and architects*, vol. 4, transl. by G. du C. de Vere, www.gutenberg.org.

Villani G., *Cronica*, Edizioni Coen, Firenze 1844.

Wey W., *Loca Sancta in Stacionibus Jerusalem*, 1485.

Monographs, Essays, Catalogs

Badde P., *The True Icon*, San Francisco, Ignatius Press, 2012.

Badde P., *The Face of God*, San Francisco, Ignatius Press, 2010.

Belting H., *La vera immagine di Cristo*, Torino, Bollati Boringhieri, 2007.

Bianchi L., *Il Sudario di Oviedo*, in "30Giorni", 4, 2009.

Bianchi L., *Il velo di Manoppello*, in "30Giorni", 4, 2009.

Bini A., in "Il Volto Santo di Manoppello", 1, 2007.

Brentano R., *Rome before Avignon: A Social History of Thirteenth-Century Rome*, Berkeley, University of California Press, 1991.

Ceresa M., *Grimaldi, Giacomo*, in *Dizionario Biografico degli Italiani*, vol. 59, Roma, Istituto dell'Enciclopedia Italiana, 2003.

Chastel A., *Il sacco di Roma. 1527*, Torino, Einaudi, 2010.

Chastel A., *La Véronique*, in "Revue de l'Art", 40/41, 1978.

Ciggaar K.N., *Une description de Constantinople dans le "Tarragonensis" 55*, in "Revue des études byzantines", 53, 1995.

Clément O., *Piccola introduzione alla teologia dell'icona*, in "Contacts", 181, 1998.

Clément O., *Via Crucis*, 10 aprile 1998 (Roma).

Di Blasio T.M., *Veronica: il mistero del Volto. Itinerari iconografici, memoria e rappresentazione*, Torino, Città Nuova, 2000.

Dobschütz E. von, *Christusbilder*, Leipzig, J.C. Hinrichs, 1899.

Evdokìmov P.N., *Teologia della bellezza*, Cinisello Balsamo, San Paolo, 1990.

Falcinelli R., *La Veronica e il Volto Santo di Manoppello. Nuovi contributi*, Atti del convegno, Frascati 2010.

Falla Castelfranchi M., *Il Mandylion nel Mezzogiorno Medioevale*, in *Intorno al Sacro Volto. Genova, Bisanzio e il Mediterraneo (secoli XI-*

XIV), a cura di A.R. Calderoni Masetti, C. Dufour Bozzo, G. Wolf, Venezia, Marsilio, 2007.

Fantaguzzi G., "Caos". Cronache cesenati del sec. XV, a cura di D. Bazzocchi, Cesena 1915.

Fanti G., *Ricerche scientifiche su immagini acheropite*, contribution to the conference on *Il Volto Santo di Manoppello*, Padova, 20 marzo 2007.

Ferrari R., *La Veronica*, in *Iconografia e arte cristiana*, a cura di L. Castelfranchi Vegas, M.A. Crippa, Cinisello Balsamo, San Paolo, 2004.

Fogliandini E., *Il volto di Cristo*, Milano, Jaca Book, 2011.

Forte B., *Il Volto Santo di Manoppello e la plausibilità teologica delle immagini acheropite*, contribution of January 25, 2007, during a conference organized by National German Television ZDF, published on April 21, 2007.

Freeman C., *Holy bones, holy dust: how relics shaped the history of medieval Europe*, New Haven (CT)-London, Yale University Press, 2012.

Frommel C.L., Wolf G. (a cura di), *L'immagine di Cristo, dall'acheropita alla mano d'artista. Dal tardo medioevo all'età barocca*, Città del Vaticano, Biblioteca Apostolica Vaticana, 2006.

Frugoni A., *Pellegrini a Roma nel 1300. Cronache del primo Giubileo*, Casale Monferrato, Piemme, 1999.

Gaeta S., *L'enigma del Volto di Gesù*, Milano, Rizzoli, 2010.

Gharib G., *La festa del Santo Mandylion nella Chiesa Bizantina*, in *La Sindone e la Scienza*, Atti del II congresso internazionale di sindonologia (Torino, 7-8 ottobre 1978), Torino, Edizioni Paoline, 1979.

Gharib G., *Le icone di Cristo*, Torino, Città Nuova, 1993.

Giussani L., *L'attrattiva Gesù*, Milano, Bur, 1999.

Giussani L., *Egli solo è*, Cinisello Balsamo, San Paolo, 2005.

Gori N., *Un canto d'amore al Volto Santo, biografia della Beata Maria Pierina De Micheli*, Città del Vaticano, Libreria Editrice Vaticana, 2012.

Gottuso C., *Il Volto Santo di Manoppello: alcune fonti storiche a confronto*, Tesi di laurea, Pontificia Università Gregoriana, Corso superiore per i Beni Culturali della Chiesa, a.a. 2003-2004, Dissertation Director H. Pfeiffer.

Grabar A., *Le vie della creazione nell'iconografia cristiana, Antichità e Medioevo*, Milano, Jaca Book, 1983.

Hamburger J.F., *The Visual and the Visionary: Art and Female Spirituality in Late Medieval Germany*, New York, Zone Books, 1998.

Jaworski J.S., Fanti G., *3-D processing to evidence characteristics represented in Manoppello veil*, in *Proceedings of the International Workshop on the Scientific approach to the Acheiropoietos Images*, Frascati, 4-6 maggio 2010.

Jaworski J.S., *Properties of byssal threads, the chemical nature of their colors and the Veil of Manoppello*, in *Proceedings of the International Workshop on the Scientific approach to the Acheiropoietos Images*, Frascati, 4-6 maggio 2010.

Laurentin R., Debroise F.M., *Indagine su Maria. Le rivelazioni dei mistici sulla vita della Madonna*, Milano, Mondadori, 2011.

L'Iconografia della SS. Trinità nel Sacro Monte di Ghiffa, Contesto e confronti, Atti del convegno internazionale, Verbania, 23-24 marzo 2007.

Lidov A., *Il Dittico del Sinai e il Mandylion*, in A.R. Calderoni Masetti, C. Dufour Bozzo, G. Wolf, *Intorno al Sacro Volto. Genova, Bisanzio e il Mediterraneo (secoli XI-XIV)*, Exhibit Catalog, Venezia, Marsilio, 2007.

Lidov A., *The miracle of reproduction: the Mandylion and Keramion as a paradigm of the sacred space*, in *L'immagine di Cristo, dall'acheropita alla mano d'artista*, a cura di C.L. Frommel, G.

Wolf, Città del Vaticano, Biblioteca Apostolica Vaticana, 2006.

Mâle E., *L'art religieux du XVIIe siècle*, Paris, Armand Colin, 1951.

Mejía J.M., *Vedere il volto di Cristo*, in *Il volto di Cristo*, a cura di G. Morello, G. Wolf, Exhibit Catalog, Milano, Electa, 2000.

Menozzi D., *La Chiesa e le immagini*, Cinisello Balsamo, San Paolo, 1995.

Montaigne M. de, *Journal de voyage en Italie*, Libr. générale française, Paris 1974.

Morello G., *Cornice trecentesca della Veronica*, in *Il volto di Cristo*, a cura di G. Morello, G. Wolf, Exhibit Catalog, Milano, Electa, 2000.

Morello G., *"Or fu sì fatta la sembianza vostra?". La Veronica di san Pietro: storia ed immagine*, in *La basilica di San Pietro. Fortuna e immagine*, a cura di G. Morello, Roma, Gangemi, 2012.

Morello G., *Opusculum de sacrosancto Veronicae Sudario et Lancea*, in *Il volto di Cristo*, a cura di G. Morello, G. Wolf, Exhibit Catalog, Milano, Electa, 2000.

Mori E., Wolf G., *Lettera dello scrittore pontificio Silvestro (cat. IV, 9)*, in *Il volto di Cristo*, a cura di G. Morello, G. Wolf, Exhibit Catalog, Milano, Electa, 2000.

Nicolotti A., *Forme e vicende del Mandilio di Edessa secondo alcune moderne interpretazioni*, in *Sacre impronte e oggetti "non fatti da mano d'uomo" nelle religioni*, a cura di A. Monaci Castagno, Atti del convegno internazionale (Torino, 18-20 maggio 2010), Alessandria, Edizioni dell'Orso, 2011.

Pearson K., *Die Fronica: ein Beitrag zur Geschichte des Christusbildes im Mittelalter*, Strasbourg, Karl J. Trübner, 1887.

Pedica S., *Il Volto Santo nei documenti della Chiesa*, Torino, Marietti, 1960.

Pfeiffer H., *Ma la "Veronica" è a Manoppello*, in "30Giorni", 5, 2000.

Pfeiffer H., Pascalis Schlömer B., Ghisetti Giavarina A., *Il Volto Santo di Manoppello*, Pescara, Carsa, 2000.

Podestà B., *Carlo V a Roma nell'anno 1536*, in "Archivio della R. Società Romana di Storia Patria", 1, 1878.

Pregare con le immagini. Il Breviario di Caterina Vigri, a cura di V. Fortunati e C. Leonardi, Firenze, Sismel, Edizioni del Galluzzo, 2004.

Ragusa I., *The Iconography of the Abgar Cycle in Paris, Ms. Lat. 2688 and Its Relationship to Byzantine Cycles*, in "Miniatura", 2, 1989.

Rajna P., *Per la data della "Vita Nuova" e non per essa soltanto*, in "Giornale Storico della Letteratura Italiana", vol. XXXVIII, Torino, Ermanno Loescher, 1901.

Rezza D., *Il "Sudario" della Veronica nella Basilica Vaticana. Storia e testimonianza di una devozione*, Città del Vaticano, Edizioni Capitolo Vaticano, 2010.

Rezza D., *Segnor mio Iesù Cristo, Dio verace, or fu sì fatta la sembianza vostra?*, in "30 Giorni", 3, 2000.

Sanvito P., *Imitatio. L'amore dell'immagine sacra. Il sentimento devoto nelle scene dell'imitazione di Cristo*, Città di Castello, Zip, 2009.

Saracino F., *Cristo a Venezia. Pittura e cristologia nel Rinascimento*, Milano-Genova, Marietti 1820, 2007.

Schiaparelli L., *Carterio di San Pietro in Vaticano*, "Archivio della R. Società Romana di Storia Patria", XXIV.

Schönborn C., *A sua immagine e somiglianza*, Torino, Lindau, 2008.

Schönborn C., *L'icona di Cristo, Fondamenti teologici*, Cinisello Balsamo, San Paolo, 1988.

Fig. 103 Petrus Christus, *Portrait of a Young Man*, c. 1464, oil on panel, detail; London, National Gallery. The hymn *Salve Sancta Facies* is written on the parchment on the wall behind the young man praying.

Scola A., *"Tu mi guardi dalla croce"*, Cristo destino dell'uomo, Belluno, 3 aprile 2004.

Smeyers M., *L'Art de la Miniature flamande du VIIIe au XVe siècle*, Tournai, La Renaissance du Livre, 1998.

Solov'ëv V., *Russia and the Universal Church*, transl. by H. Rees, London, Geoffrey Bles Ltd., 1948.

Spieser J.M., Yota E., *"Mandylion" o Sainte Face de Laon*, in *Il volto di Cristo*, a cura di G. Morello, G. Wolf, Exhibit Catalog, Milano, Electa, 2000.

Sturgis A., *The True Likeness*, in *The Image of Christ*, Exhibit Catalog *Seeing Salvation*, curator G. Finaldi, London, National Gallery Company Limited, 2000.

Tricca F., *Donato da Bomba, il primo storico del Volto Santo di Manoppello*, in "Il Volto Santo di Manoppello, Bollettino del Santuario", 1, 2011.

Vidier A., *Le trésor de la Sainte-Chapelle*, in "Mémoires de la Société de l'Histoire de Paris et de l'Île-de-France", 35, 1908.

Vittore D., contribution to the conference on *Il Volto Santo di Manoppello e l'iconografia dell'immagine di Cristo*, Università G. d'Annunzio, Chieti, febbraio 2006.

Wilson I., *La Veronica e la Sindone*, in "Il telo", I, gennaio-aprile 2000.

Wojtyła K., "Il nome", da *La redenzione cerca la tua forma per entrare nell'inquietudine di ogni uomo*, in K. Woityła, *Tutte le poesie*, Corriere della Sera, Milano 2005.

Wolf G., *"Or fu sì fatta la sembianza vostra?". Sguardi alla "vera icona" e alle sue copie artistiche*, in *Il volto di Cristo*, a cura di G. Morello, G. Wolf, Exhibit Catalog, Milano, Electa, 2000.

NOTES

[1] Robert D. Putnam, *Bowling Alone*, New York, Simon & Schuster, 2000.

[2] Ex. 20:4 and Deut. 4:15-18.

[3] Cf. Eusebio di Cesarea, *Lettera all'imperatrice Costanza*, in *Textus byzantinos ad iconomachiam pertinentes*, edited by H. Hennephof, Leiden, Brill, 1969, cited in Daniele Menozzi, *La Chiesa e le immagini*, Cinisello Balsamo, San Paolo, 1995, pp. 74-75.

[4] Giorgio di Cipro, *Nouthesia*, ed. Mélioniransky, p. 23.

[5] "Listen, brothers and fathers, and I will tell all of you who are in fear of God the things that have happened in new Bethlehem of Kamouliana, and I, humble Gregory, will place before the eyes of all the things regarding the venerable image and the blessed Bass, whose name has been changed to Aquiline, things shown to my unworthy self by the Holy Spirit:" Gregory of Nyssa, *Inventio imaginis in Camulianis*, ch. 2. Our translation.

[6] According to Alexei Lidov, the image of Christ inside a clypeus in a seventh century icon of Saints Sergius and Bacchus, originally from the Monastery of St Catherine of Sinai and kept in Kiev, could be a rare echo of the *Kamouliana*. Cf. Alexei Lidov, *Il Dittico del Sinai e il Mandylion*, in Anna Rosa Calderoni Masetti, Colette Dufour Bozzo, Gerhard Wolf, *Intorno al Sacro Volto. Genova, Bisanzio e il Mediterraneo (secoli XI-XIV)*, Exhibition catalog, Venezia, Marsilio, 2007, p. 83.

[7] Perhaps the cloak seen in Egypt in 570 by a pilgrim from Piacenza, Italy, was the *Kamouliana*. "In Memphis, we saw a cloak made of linen on which the image of the Saviour was impressed, with which, they say, at that time he dried his face, and his face remained impressed on it and is adored every day. We too adored it, but because of its splendor, we could not admire it at length, because as you gazed at it, it changed in front of your eyes" (Anonimo Piacentino, *Itinera Jerosolimitana*, XV, 44).

[8] The historian George Kedrenos wrote in 574: "The image not made by human hands has arrived from *Kamouliana*, a place in Cappadocia, and the venerable wood [of the Cross] from the city of Apamea in second Syria." Cf. Ernst von Dobschütz, *Christusbilder*, J.C. Hinrichs, Leipzig 1899, p. 125. Our translation of Heinrich Pfeiffer's translation from the Greek.

[9] Theophylactus Simocattus, *Historiae*, Book II, Ch. 3-4.

[10] *Ibid.*, libro II, cap. 4, par. 8 (p. 48).

[11] Giorgio di Pisidia, *De expeditione Heraclii imperatoris contra Persas*, libri tres, libro I, vv. 139-153. See also Theophanes: "[...] the human-divine figure, which was not drawn by human hands, but formed by the Word which forms and creates all things, with no limitation, like a pregnancy without seed. Trusting in the model that God himself designed, he commenced his battles."

[12] Sources of doubtful historical value report that the *Kamouliana* reached Rome in 705 and that the veil was superimposed on the *acheiropoieton* icon of the Savior in the Lateran Basilica, of which the earliest documents are dated 752. According to the hypothesis of Fr Heinrich Pfeiffer, the Roman Veronica could be the ancient *Kamouliana*, which was transferred towards the twelfth century from the Lateran to the Basilica of St Peter's.

[13] Vladimir Solov'ëv, *Russia and The Universal Church* (transl. by H. Rees), London, Geoffrey Bles, 1948, p. 16.

[14] Cf. Pàvel Nikolàjevič Evdokìmov, *Teologia della bellezza*, Milano, San Paolo, 1990, p. 198.

[15] Greek text in Greek Patrology 94, 1173.

[16] The Synaxarion is a collection of lives of the saints for liturgical use, equivalent to the Latin Martyrology. The Synaxarion of the Mandylion, dated around the year 1000, was presented by Georges Gharib at the 2nd international conference on Sindonology in Turin in 1978. Georges Gharib, *La festa del Santo Mandylion nella Chiesa Bizantina*, in *La Sindone e la scienza, Atti del II con-*

gresso internazionale di Sindonologia (Torino, 7-8 ottobre 1978), Torino, Edizioni Paoline, 1979.

[17] M.R. James, *The Apocryphal New Testament*, Translation and Notes, Oxford, Clarendon Press, 1924. www.pseudepigrafa.com

[18] Evagrius Scholasticus, *Ecclesiastical History*, Book IV, 27, p. 226.

[19] In the sources that describe the acquisition of the image, we read that the emperor, aware of the existence of several copies of the acheiropoieton image, had three copies sent to him before choosing the one that seemed authentic to him.

[20] Constantine VII Porphyrogenitus, Greek text in Greek Patrology 113, 454. Our translation.

[21] According to art historian André Grabar, all icons recall the *Mandylion* through the linen that the icon painter spreads on the wooden panel being painted.

[22] Olivier Clément, *Piccola introduzione alla teologia dell'icona*, in "Contacts", 181, 1998, pp. 25-32.

[23] Cf. Georges Gharib, *Le icone di Cristo*, Torino, Città Nuova, 1993, p. 53.

[24] Krijnie N. Ciggaar, *Une description de Constantinople dans le 'Tarragonensis 55'*, in "Revue des études byzantines", 53, 1995, pp. 120-121. Our translation.

[25] Robert de Clary, a Picard knight, is well-known for having made one of the first historical mentions of the Shroud of Turin as being among the relics of Constantinople.

[26] Robert de Clary, *The Conquest of Constantinople*, transl. by Edgar Holmes McNeal, NY, Norton, 1969, pp. 90-91.

[27] *Ibid.*

[28] In 1978 the English writer Ian Wilson hypothesized that the Mandylion could actually be the Shroud of Turin. As Georges Gharib said, "this is an undoubtedly attractive hypothesis, because it would fill the gaps in the history of the Shroud. But the proposal stalls against the fact that according to the most ancient traditions – both literary and iconographic – the *Mandylion* showed only the face of Christ and not his whole body. Moreover, the *Mandylion* is not a funeral portrait, unlike the Shroud. (Gharib, *Le icone di Cristo*, op. cit., p. 57. Our translation). The hypothesis is still being debated. See, for example, Andrea Nicolotti, *Forme e vicende del Mandilio di Edessa secondo alcune moderne interpretazioni*, in *Sacre impronte e oggetti "non fatti da mano d'uomo" nelle religioni*, edited by Adele Monaci Castagno, Atti del convegno internazionale (Torino, 18-20 maggio 2010), Alessandria, Edizioni dell'Orso, 2011, pp. 279-304.

[29] Cf. Alexei Lidov, "The miracle of reproduction: the Mandylion and Keramion as a paradigm of the sacred space", in *L'immagine di Cristo, dall'acheropita alla mano d'artista*, edited by Christoph L. Frommel and Gerhard Wolf, Città del Vaticano, Biblioteca Apostolica Vaticana, 2006, pp. 17-41.

[30] The sources that define the Oratorio of Santa Maria al Presepe as "Sanctae Mariae in Beronica" are the oldest witness accounts of the presence of a *sudarium* in St Peter's. Benedict, a monk from Sant'Andrea sul Soratte, reports in his chronicle written around the year 1000: "Johannes [...] papa [...] fecit oratorium sancte Dei genitricis, opere pulcherrimo intra ecclesiam beati Petri apostoli, ubi dicitur a Veronice" (*Monumenta Germaniae Historica, Scriptores*, III, p. 700). In an act dated 1018, we find the signature "Johannes vir magnificus clerico et mansionario Sanctae Mariae in Beronica" (Luigi Schiaparelli, *Carterio di San Pietro in Vaticano*, "Archivio della R. Società Romana di Storia Patria", XXIV, pp. 451-453).

[31] Cf. Gerhard Wolf, "*Or fu sì fatta la sembianza vostra?*". *Sguardi alla "vera icona" e alle sue copie artistiche*, in *Il volto di Cristo*, edited by Giovanni Morello and Gerhard Wolf, Exhibit Catalog, Milano, Electa, 2000, p. 103.

[32] In Baluze, *Epist. Inn.*, III, II, 99 (ep. 179);

Coll. Bull. SS. Eccl. Vat., I, 89. Cited in Pio Rajna, *Per la data della "Vita Nuova" e non per essa soltanto*, in "Giornale Storico della Letteratura Italiana", vol. XXXVIII, Torino, Ermanno Loescher, 1901.

[33] The dogma of Transubstantiation was proclaimed by Innocent III in 1215. The Feast of Corpus Domini, first held in Belgium in 1247, was extended to the whole Church by Urban IV in 1264.

[34] "Dum vero fortunalis alea statum Regni Angliae talibus turbinibus exagitaret, dominus Papa Innocentius, quem vacillantis Ecclesiae cura sollicitabat, effigiem vultus Domini, quae Veronica dicitur, ut moris est, de ecclesia Sancti Petri versus hospitale Sancti Spiritus reverenter cum processione baiulabat. Qua peracta, ipsa effigies, dum in locum suum apportaretur, se per se gyrabat, ut verso staret ordine, ita scilicet, ut frons inferius, barba superius locaretur. Quod nimis abhorrens dominus Papa, credidit illud in triste sibi praesagium evenisse, et ut plenius Deo reconciliaretur, Consilio fratrum, in honorem ipsius effigii, quae Veronica dicitur, quandam orationem composuit elegantem, cui adiecit quondam Psalmum, cum quibusdam versiculis; et eadem dicentibus, decem dierum concessit indulgentiam, ita scilicet, ut quotiescumque repetatur toties dicenti tantundem indulgentiae concedatur" (Matthew Paris, *Chronica Majora*).

[35] Jerome, *Commentary on Matthew*, Ch. 21, v. 15. On the topic of the power of a gaze, Francesco Saracino recalls the importance of ancient and medieval theories of active vision, the luminous pneuma which emanates from the eyes towards the object being looked at. Cf. Francesco Saracino, *Cristo a Venezia, Pittura e cristologia nel Rinascimento*, Milano-Genova, Marietti 1820, 2007, pp. 45-52.

[36] Mt 9:36

[37] Mk 10:21

[38] Lk 22:61-62. Cf. Ambrogio, *Expositio Evangelii secundum Lucam*, 10: 88-90: "Peter was saddened and wept because he went wrong like all men. It is not known what he said, but that he wept [...] Peter denied once, but did not weep, because the Lord had not looked at him; he denied a second time, but did not cry because the Lord had not yet looked at him. He denied a third time; Jesus looked at him and he wept most bitterly. Look at us, Lord Jesus, that we may weep over our sin."

[39] From the popularised version written in the 1400s by Gérard de Frachet, *Le "Vitae fratrum" di Geraldo Frachet dei Predicatori*, edited by A. Ferrua, Bologna, Tamari, 1963, p. 219, cited in Saracino, *Cristo a Venezia*, op. cit., p. 47.

[40] Gertrude of Helfta, *Legatus Divinae Pietatis*, IV, 7.

[41] Jeffrey F. Hamburger, *The Visual and the Visionary: Art and Female Spirituality in Late Medieval Germany*, New York, Zone Book, 1998, p. 318.

[42] Mechthild von Hackeborn, *Liber specialis gratiae*, 1291.

[43] Dante Alighieri, *Vita Nova*, transl. by Mark Musa, Bloomington, Indiana University Press, 1965.

[44] "Deus, qui nobis signatis lumine vultus tui memoriale tuum ad instantiam Veronicae sudario impressam imaginem relinquere voluisti, per passionem et crucem tuam tribue nobis quaesumus, ut ita nunc in terris per speculum et in aenigmate ipsam adorare et venerari valeamus, ut facie ad faciem venientem iudicem te securi videamus" (Oh God, who marked us with the light of Your Face, and on Veronica's request, as a memory, you left us Your Image imprinted on the sudarium; grant, we beg you, by your passion and death, that we may adore you, venerate you, in mysterious and mirror-like fashion on earth, that we may certainly see you, face to face, when you come as our judge), in Stefano Pedica, *Il Volto Santo nei documenti della Chiesa*, Torino, Marietti, 1960, p. 140.

[45] Cf. Lk 8:43-48.

[46] *The Golden Legend or Lives of the Saints*. Com-

piled by Jacobus de Voragine, Archbishop of Genoa, 1275. First Edition Published 1470. Englished by William Caxton, First Edition 1483, Edited by F.S. Ellis, Temple Classics, 1900. Scanned by Robert Blackmon for the Internet Medieval Source Book, Fordham University Center for Medieval Studies. Vol 1. The Passion of our Lord. www.fordham.edu/halsall/basis/goldenlegend/

[47] *Ibid.*

[48] In Bordeaux the Church of Saint-Seurin has been associated with prayers to Veronica since the 12th/13th century.

[49] "Oratorium Sanctae Genitricis Virginis Mariae quod vocatur Veronica, ubi sine dubio est Sudarium Christi, in quo ante passionem suam sanctissimam faciem, ut a maioribus accepimus, extersit, quando sudor ejus factus est sicut guttae sanguinis decurrentis in terram" (The oratory of the Holy Mother of God, called Veronica, where undoubtedly is the Sudarium of Christ, on which before his passion, as we know from the ancients, he wiped his holy face, when his sweat became like drops of blood which fell to the ground), in Jean Mabillon, *Museum Italicum*, II, 122.

[50] *Merlin and the Grail: Joseph of Arimathea, Merlin, Perceval: the trilogy of prose romances attributed to Robert de Boron*, translated by Nigel Bryant, Cambridge, D.S. Brewer, 2001, p. 28.

[51] Cf. Emanuela Fogliandini, *Il volto di Cristo*, Milano, Jaca Book, 2011, p. 173.

[52] "Lap strat di trivium flent sudar sincopizavit Por pis lap que schola domus her Symonis Pharisey. 1. Lap/lapis: the stone with the crosses on top on which Christ fell with the cross. 2. Strat/strata: the path Christ took during the Passion. 3. Di/divitis: house of the rich man who refused to give Lazarus any scraps. 4. Trivium: the trivium where Christ fell with the cross. 5. Flent: the place where the women wept over Christ. 6. Sudar/sudarium: the place where a widow or Veronica placed a sudarium on Christ's face 7. Sincopizavit: place where the blessed Virgin Mary sobbed. 8. Por/ gate Christ went through during his passion. 9. Pis/pool in which the sick were healed during Christ's time. 10. Lap/lapides: stones Christ stood on when he was condemned to death. 11. Shola/ scholas: place where the Blessed Virgin Mary went to school. 12. Domus: Pilate's house. 13. Her/Hernias: Herod's house. 14. Symonis Pharisey: House of Simon the Pharisee." In William Wey, Loca Sancta in Stacionibus Jerusalem, 1485.

[53] Cf. Wolf, "*Or fu sì fatta la sembianza vostra?*", *op. cit.*, p. 105.

[54] Bonifacio VIII, Bolla pontificia *Antiquorum habet fide relatio*.

[55] Gaetano Moroni, *Dizionario di erudizione storico-ecclesiastica*, Venezia, Tipografia Emiliana, 1840-1861.

[56] Card. Iacopo Gaetano Stefaneschi, *De centesimo seu Jubileo anno liber*, trad. Modestino Cerra, in Arsenio Frugoni, *Pellegrini a Roma nel 1300*, Casale Monferrato, Piemme, 1999.

[57] *Ibid.*

[58] *Ibid.*

[59] Cf. Elisabetta Mori, Gerhard Wolf, "*Lettera dello scrittore pontificio Silvestro*" (cat. IV, 9), in *Il volto di Cristo*, *op. cit.*, pp. 176-178.

[60] Giovanni Villani, *Cronica*, VIII, 26, Firenze, Edizioni Coen, 1844.

[61] Stefaneschi, *De Centesimo seu jubileo anno liber*, *op. cit.*

[62] Frugoni, *Pellegrini a Roma nel 1300*, *op. cit.*, pp. 54-55; 65.

[63] Dante, *Inferno*, XVIII, vv. 28-33. Translated by Robert Hollander and Jean Hollander. Princeton Dante Project.

[64] Robert Brentano, *Rome before Avignon, A Social History of Thirteenth-Century Rome*, Berkeley-Los Angeles, University of California Press, 1991.

[65] The Flemish painter Petrus Christus depicts

him on parchment behind a young pilgrim at the Jubilee of 1350.

[66] Francesco Petrarca, *Il Canzoniere XVI*, transl. by A.S. Kline, 2002.

[67] Benedetto XII, *Costituzione Benedictus Deus*: DS 1000-1001.

[68] "Salve nostrum gaudium / in hac vita dura / labili et fragili / cito peritura; / o felix figura / ad videndam Faciem / que est Christi pura / nos deduc ad propria". *Salve Santa Facies*, in Pedica, *Il Volto Santo nei documenti della Chiesa*, op. cit., pp. 133-136.

[69] Quoted in Saverio Gaeta, *L'enigma del Volto di Gesù*, Milano, Rizzoli, 2010, p. 24.

[70] Giorgio Vasari, *Life of Ugo da Carpi*.

[71] Cf. Giovanni Morello, *Cornice trecentesca della Veronica*, in *Il volto di Cristo*, op. cit., p. 205.

[72] In his study on the Veronica (Karl Pearson, *Die Fronica: ein Beitrag zur Geschichte des Christusbildes im Mittelalter*, Strasbourg, Karl J. Trübner, 1887), the author suggests it could represent the color *celicus*, the color of the sky that flows forth from Christ's face.

[73] *Ibid*.

[74] This hypothesis was also suggested by Giovanni Morello in *"Or fu sì fatta la sembianza vostra?". La Veronica di San Pietro: storia ed immagine*, in *La basilica di San Pietro. Fortuna e immagine*, edited by Giovanni Morello, Roma, Gangemi, 2012, p. 78.

[75] Giacomo Grimaldi, *Opusculum de sacrosancto Veronicae Sudario*.

[76] The icon also bears the paleo-Slavic inscription "Portrait of the Savior on the Mandylion", which was thought to be Greek or Jewish until the arrival of the Tsar, Peter the Great. Because of this relic, the convent became a pilgrimage center. The icon was latterly donated to Laon Cathedral, where it can still be found in the Chapel of St Thomas Beckett.

[77] Cf. Jean-Michel Spieser, Elisabeth Yota, *"Mandylion" o Sainte Face de Laon*, in *Il volto di Cristo*, op. cit., p. 97.

[78] Alexander Vidier, *Le trésor de la Sainte-Chapelle*, in "Mémoires de la Société de l'Histoire de Paris et de l'Île-de-France", 35, 1908, p. 193 (inventory M).

[79] *Ibid.*, pp. 190-192. For the *Mandylion* in Paris, see Nicolotti, *Forme e vicende del Mandilio di Edessa secondo alcune moderne interpretazioni*, op. cit.

[80] Martin Luther, *Wider das Papsttum zu Rom, vom Teufel gestiftet* (1545), WA 54, 228-263.

[81] As Hamburger points out, the mystics Gertrude of Helfta, Mechthild of Hackeborn and Julian of Norwich offer the most ancient and wide-ranging comments on the Roman Veronica. It is strange that none of these texts are cited in the monumental history of the image by Ernst von Dobschütz nel 1899 (*Immagini di Cristo*, Napoli, Medusa, 2006), which has so far been considered as the fundamental text for studies of the Holy Face. Cfr. Hamburger, *The Visual and the Visionary*, op. cit., p. 351.

[82] Julian of Norwich, *Divine Revelations of Love*, Second Revelation, Chapter X. (www.ccel.org)

[83] The arrival of the Holy Shroud in the West, with its blood marks on the forehead and head, may also have influenced the new representation of the Veronica.

[84] Cf. C. Freeman, *Holy bones, holy dust: how relics shaped the history of medieval Europe*, New Haven (CT)-London, Yale University Press, 2012.

[85] Cf. *Imago pietatis con Maria e Maria Maddalena*, Maestro della Madonna Strauss, 1400, Galleria dell'Accademia, Firenze.

[86] Medieval artists vied with each other in drawing signs and symbols from the Gospel accounts of the Passion. Extrapolated from their narrative context, these signs were used as ways of jogging one's memory, or starting points for meditation: a face spitting, a hand that strikes, a crown of thorns, wounds, a bucket of vinegar, a stick with the

sponge on the end of it, a blindfold, a hammer, three nails, pincers, thirty pieces of silver, bloody footprints, a stick, a whip, a ladder, a seamless garment, three dice, a spear, etc. The symbolic character of the instruments transformed them into a sort of heraldic coat of arms: the Arms of Christ, the emblems of Salvation.

[87] From the mid-13th century, representations and prayers linked to the image in Rome not made by human hands appear in Breviaries and Books of Hours, as well as in other books for the liturgy and texts of various types. After the invention of printing, this habit of prayer continued for a while also through woodcuts. See the site "Veronica Books", which lists the different types of books containing miniatures of the Holy Face.

[88] Think, for example, of the Mass for St Gregory which had a great following after the institution of the Feast of Corpus Domini in 1247. Here the Veronica appears often next to a consecrated host. [cf. fig. 15].

[89] London, British Library, ms. Royal 6 E VI.

[90] Cambridge, Corpus Christi College, ms. 16II, Matthew Paris, Chronica Majora, II, XIII century, f. 53v. See James le Palmer, *Omne Bonum*, in *Il volto di Cristo*, op. cit., pp. 174-176.

[91] London, British Library, ms. Add. 74236. An angel holding up the holy Sudarium also appears within another initial of the same manuscript (f. 216), within the Mass of the Resurrection.

[92] See the cistercian Psalterium of the 15th century, kept in Copenhagen, at Det Kongelige Bibliotek. ms. Thott 117, loose sheet inserted between the cover and the first page. Cf. Hamburger, *The Visual and the Visionary*, op. cit., pp. 323-329.

[93] An example is kept in Paris at the Bibliothèque Nationale (Arsenal), ms. 1176, XV secolo, f. Av.

[94] For comparisons between the *Mandylion* and the Veronica, see Wolf, *"Or fu sì fatta la sembianza vostra?"*, op. cit., pp. 103-35 and Isa Ragusa, *The Iconography of the Abgar Cycle in Paris, Ms. Lat. 2688 and Its Relationship to Byzantine Cycles*, in "Miniatura", 2, 1989, pp. 35-51. For the association between il *Mandylion* and the Eucharist see Marina Falla Castelfranchi, *Il Mandylion nel Mezzogiorno Medioevale* in *Intorno al Sacro Volto. Genova, Bisanzio il Mediterraneo (secoli XI-XIV)*, edited by Anna Rosa Calderoni Masetti, Colette Dufour Bozzo, Gerhard Wolf, Venezia, Marsilio, 2007, pp. 191-193.

[95] See, for example, what is considered the oldest copy of the Roman Veronica. This is an image of Christ between Saints Peter and Paul that is contained in the pergamena with the text of the Bull instituting the Jubilee Year of 1300 (Cortona, Biblioteca del Comune e dell'Accademia Etrusca, Lettera dello scrittore pontificio Silvestro). Cf. Mori, Wolf, *Lettera dello scrittore pontificio Silvestro*, op. cit., pp. 176-78.

[96] New Haven, Yale University, Beinecke Rare Book and Manuscript Library, ms. 391, *Fasti christianae religionis* di Ludovico Lazzarelli, end XV century, f. 41.

[97] One of the many well-preserved examples one can point to is the elaborate French Book of Hours belonging to Louis de Laval. The Holy Face appears in such book many times, showing the widespread devotion to it. (Paris, Bibliothèque Nationale, ms. Lat. 920, Jean Colombe, c. 1470-1475, ff. 44, 114v, 293, 295v, 296v, 297).

[98] In this regard, see the precious work by Karl Pearson, *Die Fronica, ein Beitrag zur Geschichte des Christusbildes im Mittelalter*, Strasbourg, Karl J. Trübner, 1887.

[99] Pope John XXII even granted an indulgence of ten thousand days in connection with this hymn. He thus contributed to spreading the invocation throughout Europe, by heaving it translated and included in Books of Hours.

[100] Los Angeles, The J. Paul Getty Museum, ms. 2, Master of Guillebert de Mets, 1450-1455, f. 13v.

The iconography of the woman who had received the veil bearing the imprint of Christ's face spread across Europe from the 13th century on, whereas it did not exist in Byzantine art. An interesting article in this regard was written by Isa Ragusa (*Iconography, op. cit.*, pp. 35-51) on the rich manuscript with 22 miniatures of a Latin version of the cycle of King Abgarus (Paris, Bibliothèque Nationale, ms. Lat. 2688), which was probably made in Rome in the second half of the 13th century. In one of these miniatures, in order to save the *Mandylion*, King Abgarus' widow takes it to Jerusalem, and then finally reaches Rome (f. 96). This scene is not present in other Byzantine illuminated manuscripts and, in Ragusa's view, should be linked up with the Latin legends about Veronica, such as the one about the healing of Tiberius (*Cura sanitatis Tiberii*).

[101] Cf. Paolo Sanvito, *Imitatio. L'amore dell'immagine sacra. Il sentimento devoto nelle scene dell'imitazione di Cristo*, Città di Castello, Zip, 2009, pp. 13-34. Compared to images abroad, few manuscripts preserved in Italian libraries have been published online. It is hoped that, as knowledge spreads, more examples of depictions of the Veronica will be found in Italy too. Some are known, particularly in the North, such as the ones in the Lombardy Book of Hours of Bona Sforza (London, British Library, ms. Add. 34294, Giovan Pietro Birago, 1490-1504, f. 26); in a book of prayers for monastic use (Varese, Archivio Monastero Santa Maria del Monte, Fondo Marliani, ms. 2, c. 1500, ff. 90-90v); in the Graduale della Biblioteca Estense di Modena, which comes from the Convent of the Olivetani di San Michele in Bosco in Bologna (ms. Lat. 1013, Antonio Maria Sforza o Cristoforo da Lendinara, second half of the XV secolo, f. 67); and in the Breviary of St Caterina Vigri kept in the Monastery of Corpus Domini in Bologna (cfr. *Pregare con le immagini. Il Breviario di Caterina Vigri*, edited by Vera Fortunati and Claudio Leonardi, Firenze, Sismel, Ediz. del Galluzzo, 2004).

[102] See, for example, the Face-portrait in the Book of Hours made in Bruges, Belgium around 1450 (New York, Pierpont Morgan Library, ms. M. 421, f. 13v), which copies a Jan van Eyck model (cfr. Maurits Smeyers, *L'Art de la Miniature flamande du VIIIe au XVIe siècle*, Tournai, La Renaissance du Livre, 1998, p. 263). This started the spreading of the *Salvator mundi* iconography which, starting from the second half of the 1400s, often accompanies the hymn, *Salve Sancta Facies*.

[103] The sorrowful Holy Face is also included in pre-existent iconographies, such as *Imago pietatis* or *Arma Christi*. An early example of Veronica offering her veil to Christ along Calvary is in an English Book of Hours from the first half of the 14th century (London, British Library, ms. Egerton 2781, "Neville of Hornby Hours", f. 153v).

[104] Los Angeles, The J. Paul Getty Museum, ms. Ludwig IX 18, Master of James IV of Scotland, Book of Hours, 1510-1520, f.8v.

[105] Cf. Massimo Ceresa, *Grimaldi, Giacomo*, in *Dizionario Biografico degli Italiani*, vol. 59, Roma, Istituto dell'Enciclopedia Italiana, 2003, pp. 516-518.

[106] Other copies exist that are not original manuscripts, written in the following years, such as the one by Francesco Speroni, dating from 1635, kept in the Vatican Library.

[107] The date of 705 is accepted by G. Morello: cf. his papers in G. Wolf, *"Or fu sì fatta la sembianza vostra?". Sguardi alla "vera icona" e alle sue copie artistiche*, in *Il volto di Cristo*, Milano, Electa, 2000, pp. 103-211; see also his contribution entitled *"Or fu sì fatta la sembianza vostra?". La Veronica di San Pietro. Storia e immagine*, in *La basilica di San Pietro. Fortuna e immagine*, Roma 2012, pp. 39-80: 45-46.

[108] This is what M. Cerrati says in his footnotes to Tiberii Alpharani *De basilicae Vaticanae antiquis-*

sima et nova structura, Roma 1914, p. 107. Cerrati's source is the famous archeologist, Giovanni Battista De Rossi.

[109] Morello, *Opusculum de sacrosancto Veronicae Sudario et Lancea* in *Il volto di Cristo, op. cit.*, p. 210.

[110] *Ibid.*

[111] Giuliano Fantaguzzi, *"Caos". Cronache cesenati del sec. XV*, edited by D. Bazzocchi, Cesena, 1915, p. 268.

[112] Cf. Marin Sanudo, *I Diarii*, edited by R. Fulin, F. Stefani, N. Barozzi, G. Berchet, M. Allegri, Venezia 1879-1903, 58 voll., vol. XLV, col. 122.

[113] *Die warhafftige und kurtze Berichtung*, cited in André Chastel, *Il sacco di Roma. 1527*, Torino, Einaudi, 2010, p. 79.

[114] Grimaldi, *Opusculum, op. cit.*

[115] "He listened to Paul III's pontifical mass in St Peter's and venerated the Holy Face and the holy iron of the Lance. He left from Rome on the 18th of that month, kissing its holy feet", in Francesco Maria Torrigio, *Le Sacre Grotte*, Roma 1639², vol. II, p. 109. See also Bartolomeo Podestà, *Carlo V a Roma nell'anno 1536*, in "Archivio della R. Società Romana di Storia Patria", 1, 1878, p. 339.

[116] Angelo Pientini, *Le Pie Narrationi delle opere più memorabili fatte in Roma l'anno del giubileo 1575*, translation by Agostino Colaldo, Viterbo 1577, pp. 69; 178-179.

[117] Cf. Hans Belting, *La vera immagine di Cristo*, Torino, Bollati Boringhieri, 2007, p. 139.

[118] This decision was contested by the Bollandists in Belgium.

[119] A. Bahlet, *Le vite dei Santi e la storia delle feste dell'anno*, Parigi 1703, t. IV, coll. 21-28.

[120] Emile Mâle, *L'art religieux du XVIIᵉ siècle*, Paris, Armand Colin, 1951, pp. 103 ff.

[121] André Chastel attributes the loss of the features on Christ's face to the artists' trauma brought about by the sack of Rome. Cf. Chastel, *Il sacco di Roma, op. cit.*, pp. 142-162.

[122] Michel de Montaigne, *Journal de voyage en Italie*, Paris, Libr. générale française, 1974, pp. 293 ff.

[123] G. Grimaldi, *Instrumenta autentica translationum ss. Corpum et sacrarum reliquiarum e veteri in novam basilicam*, 1621.

[124] A similar concept is expressed by the mechanical lift which rises to the Sacred Nail placed at the top of the arch above the choir in Milan Cathedral.

[125] As the hymn *Salve Sancta Facies* says: "Ille color celicus, / qui in te splendescit, / in eodem permanet / statu nec decrescit; / diuturno tempore / minime pallescit, / fecit te Rex glorie, / fallere qui nescit. / Nesciens putredinem, / servans incorruptum" ("That heavenly colour which shines in thee remains thus for ever more and does not diminish; age after age it never fades: the King of Glory, who knows no defect, made you. Knowing no decay, and preserved incorrupt").

[126] Tiziana Maria Di Blasio, *Veronica: il mistero del Volto. Itinerari iconografici, memoria e rappresentazione*, Torino, Città Nuova, 2000, pp. 61-62.

[127] *L'Iconografia della SS. Trinità nel Sacro Monte di Ghiffa, Contesto e confronti*, Atti del convegno internazionale (Verbania, 23-24 marzo 2007), edited by Claudio Silvestri, Gravellona Toce, Tipografia Press Grafica, 2008, p. 132.

[128] When the architect Domenico Fontana finally completed the vaults in St Peter's, the huge pillars by Michelangelo under the huge dome were completely bare. Bernini had the idea of turning them into shrines for the main relics held in the basilica. He used the small Solomonic columns of the Constantine sacellum as little loggias for displaying the relics. The columns would later become the model for the ones he made from melted bronze for the ciborium. Four big statues pointed

to the relics: he himself carved the statue of St Longinus (relic: the Holy Lance) and he drew St Andrew (relic: head of the saint), St Helena (relic: fragment of the True Cross) and the Veronica, which was to be sculpted by Francesco Mochi.

[129] Cf. Marie de Saint-Pierre, *Vie de la soeur Marie de Saint-Pierre de la Sainte-Famille*, Tours, Oratoire de la Sainte-Face, 1958.

[130] Cf. Christoph Schönborn, *A sua immagine e somiglianza*, Torino, Lindau, 2008, p. 85.

[131] Consider the propagation of the devotion to the image of the Merciful Jesus by St Mary Faustina Kowalska and the spread of the devotion to the Holy Face by Blessed Maria Pierina de Micheli and Blessed Maria Pia Mastena.

[132] According to Tiziana di Blasio, "During a conversation in June 2000, Mgr. Vittorio Lanzani, secretary of Cardinal Noè, prefect of the Vatican basilica, notices that at the moment it is impossible to see even the slightest trace of human features on the relic. The visible surface of the relic is dark brown without any significant veins. It has been reported as well that a commission was established in order to study the current conditions of the 'Veronica' and to define the constitutive elements" (Di Blasio, *Veronica: il mistero*, op. cit., p. 62).

[133] Cf. Arsenio Frugoni, *La Veronica nostra*, in Id., *Pellegrini a Roma nel 1300*, op. cit., p. 88. See also Di Blasio, *Veronica: il mistero*, op. cit., p. 81, "I have insisted with the ecclesiastical authorities of the Vatican Basilica, and repeatedly requested, even in writing, and with the approval of scholars qualified to carry out historical and artistic research, that I be allowed to observe the relic of the Veronica directly. Unfortunately I have not received permission."

[134] Ian Wilson, *Veronica and the Holy Shroud*, in "Il telo", I, January-April 2000, pp. 14-16. Even those who have been able to see the Veronica recently, including the journalists Paul Badde, Saverio Gaeta and the photographer Roberto Falcinelli, described the relic as indecipherable. Cf. Roberto Falcinelli, *La Veronica e il Volto Santo di Manoppello: Nuovi Contributi*, Atti del convegno, Frascati 2010. Cf. also Paul Badde, *The Face of God*, San Francisco, Ignatius Press, 2010, Ch. 14 and following.

[135] Maria Valtorta, *L'Evangelo come mi è stato rivelato*, Vol. X, Isola del Liri, Centro Editoriale Valtortiano, 1975.

[136] Maria Valtorta, *Il Poema dell'Uomo-Dio*, vol. IX, Isola del Liri, Centro Editoriale Valtortiano, 1986, p. 333, note 20.

[137] Following an assault, Maria Valtorta (1897-1961) became paralysed in 1934. From 1943 to 1953 she had visions of the life of Jesus and Mary, which she described in 15,000 pages of a notebook. In 1956 *Il Poema dell'Uomo-Dio* (The Poem of the Man God) was published. The work, which received a warm welcome from the public, was listed in 1956 in the Index, before its abolition in 1966. The Congregation for the Doctrine of the Faith allowed the book to be re-edited and printed, as long as in the first pages it was specified that the "visions" were not thought to be supernatural, but had to be considered as literary forms which the Author used to narrate the life of Jesus, in her own way. The welcome this very long work has received from the Christian public is quite remarkable: it has been translated into 4 languages and between 1978 and 2008 sold 1,5 million copies. Cf. René Laurentin and François-Michel Debroise, *Indagine su Maria. Le rivelazioni dei mistici sulla vita della Madonna*, Milano, Mondadori, 2011, pp. 25-30.

[138] Alexandrina Maria da Costa (1904-1955), *Dai diari*, 7th September 1947.

[139] Wolf, *"Or fu sì fatta la sembianza vostra?"*, op. cit., p. 114.

[140] Jorge M. Mejía, *Vedere il volto di Cristo*, in *Il volto di Cristo*, op. cit., p. 15.

[141] Rosanna Ferrari, *La Veronica*, in *Iconografia e*

arte cristiana, edited by Liana Castelfranchi Vegas and Maria Antonietta Crippa, Cinisello Balsamo, San Paolo, 2004, vol. 2, p. 1394. See also Alexander Sturgis, *The True Likeness*, in *The Image of Christ*, catalogue of the exhibition *Seeing Salvation*, edited by Gabriele Finaldi, London, National Gallery Company Limited, 2000, p. 75.

[142] Benedict XVI, *supra*, pp. 96 ff.

[143] The date of the *Relatione* by da Bomba is not certain. In the final part of the original text in Manoppello, the author writes, "at present it is 1643". In the first pages of the document, Marzia Leonelli is mentioned as being still alive, but according to research in the archives, her death can be dated February 4th, 1643. The text should therefore precede that date. Among the miraculous healings attributed to the Holy Face in the final part of the *Relatione*, there is mention of "a man named Carlo di Anterdicio, who in the year 1643, taking a wife, was bewitched out of envy". After being taken by his relatives to Manoppello and having worshipped the Holy Face, the text continues, the man "found that he was totally healthy and free from all pain […], and as a consequence of so much grace he had several children from his wife; even today he never tires of the grace God gave him through our most holy image". The reference to the "several children" born after 1643 would imply that the account was written – or at least this part, which could have been added later – at least in 1644-45, but in any case before 1649, the year in which Da Bomba died. (Here and in the following notes from sixteenth century mss. the usual criteria of modernized spelling and punctuation will be adopted).

[144] [Donato da Bomba OFM Cap.], *Relatione historica d'una miracolosa imagine del volto di Christo signor nostro passionato*, L'Aquila, Archivio provinciale F.M. Cap., pp. 11-13 (numbered from pages 1-25, from ff. 27-54, after which follow 7 unnumbered ff).

[145] [Donato da Bomba OFM Cap.], *Vera historia et breve relatione d'una miracolosa imagine del volto di Cristo*, Manoppello, Convent OFM Cap., f. 7v.

[146] [da Bomba OFM Cap.], *Relatione historica, op. cit.*, p. 20.

[147] *Ibid.*, p. 21.

[148] *Ibid.*, f. 54r.

[149] The Holy Face from the Abruzzi is mentioned, among others, by Gaetano Moroni, *Dizionario di erudizione storico-ecclesiastica*, vol. 103, Venezia, Tipografia Emiliana, 1861, p. 109.

[150] Cf. Heinrich Pfeiffer, *Ma la "Veronica" è a Manoppello*, in "30Giorni", 5, 2000, pp. 78-79. Heinrich Pfeiffer, Blandina Pascalis Schlömer, Adriano Ghisetti Giavarina, *Il Volto Santo di Manoppello*, Pescara, Carsa, 2000.

[151] Filippo da Tussio, *Memorie storiche del Volto Santo*, L'Aquila, Tipografia Vecchioni, 1875, p. VIII, note 2.

[152] It has been said that the two manuscripts bear the date 1645: however, it is worth noting that their dating is not certain. After checking the code signed "N. from N." it appears that in the introduction "A' pii e devoti lettori" (to pious and devout readers) it is said that, regarding the *Relatione*, "verace ella promette d'essere, che però, provata che fu per publica voce et fama et per fedelissimi testimonii singolari, è stata per atti publici in detta terra di Manoppello autenticata" (it seems to be true, and therefore has been proved both by public acclaim and by faithful individual witnesses, and was authenticated in the above-mentioned territory of Manoppello by a notary's act). Since the authentication mentioned in the text, which is kept with the manuscript itself, was only performed (as previously said) in April 1646, then the drafting of the code should be moved after that date. A further matter, which cannot be examined here, would be to establish the relation between the date of the writing of the introduction and that of the text of the *Relatione*.

[153] Tussio, *Memorie storiche del Volto Santo*, op. cit., p. VIII, note 2.

[154] The text stops at the words "molti heretici et altri infedeli, li quali dicono che si commette idolatria adorandosi l'imagini di Dio huomo o pur[e] de' santi suoi, mentre in quelle non s'adora la materia della quale è fatta l'im[a]gine, ma quel Dio e quel santo o s[an]ta che ci rappresenta. Et così dicono li sa[cri] teologi" ("many heretics and other miscredents, who say that it is idolatry to adore images of God-man and of his saints, whereas in such images what is adored is not the stuff of which the image is made, but that God or saint which it represents. Thus say the holy theologians"). Between square brackets integrations to the text have been made where the original text was missing.

[155] *Vera historia et breve relatione d'una miracolosa imagine del volto di Cristo Signor nostro appassionato, quale di presente si ritrova nel convento de' pp. Cappuccini di Manoppello*, instead of *Relatione historica d'una miracolosa imagine del volto di Christo signor nostro passionato, qual al presente si ritrova nel convento de' Padri Capuccini di Manoppello, terra in Abruzzo provintia del Regno di Napoli* (this is the title that immediately precedes the *incipit* of the text; but in the mss. drawn up by Ambrogio da Pescara, the first foglio has the following caption *Vera et breve relatione historica d'una miracolosa figura over imagine del volto di Christo Signor nostro passionato et tormentato, qual al presente si ritrova nel convento de' Padri Capuccini di Manoppello, terra in Abbruzzo citra provintia del Regno di Napoli*).

[156] Cf. *supra*, note 143.

[157] Fragments of a sheet have been glued on the versus of the front plate of the parchment binding, where parts of a draft of the text of the *Relatione historica* are recognizable.

[158] The copies of the *Relatione* – except the third one mentioned here – were the subjects of Claudia Gottuso's dissertation, *Il Volto Santo di Manoppello: alcune fonti storiche a confronto*, Pontifical Gregorian University, Course in History and Cultural Heritage of the Church, 2003-2004, supervisor Heinrich Pfeiffer.

[159] The Shroud arrived at Oviedo in 840, brought by the king of Asturias Alfonso II the Chaste (791-842). In order to preserve it, he built within the royal palace the Camara Santa (Holy Chamber - at present it is part of San Salvador Cathedral). Ongoing scientific investigations seem to confirm the tradition that says that the Shroud is the cloth which was used, according to the Jewish tradition, to cover Jesus' face when he was moved from the cross to the tomb, but it was taken off his face before the Shroud was put in place. Because it was actually soaked with blood, it was left in the tomb. It was confirmed that the cloth was folded and placed on the face of a man who was already dead, and tacked behind his head. Mirror-like stains on both sides of the folded cloth have turned out to be made of blood and edematous pulmonary fluid, a substance that accumulates in the lungs when death is caused by suffocation, such as occurs after crucifixion. Fingerprints also can be distinguished among the stains, located around the mouth and nose, left probably by those who were trying to stop a flow of blood from the nose after the cloth was wrapped around the head. The stains on the *Sudarium* also show geometric correspondence with those of the Shroud. The imprint of the nose, measured both on the Shroud and the Sudarium, was found to have the same length of eight centimeters. The blood of the Oviedo *Sudarium* belongs to group AB, common in the Middle East but rare in Europe, the same group as the blood on the Shroud. The material from which the object is made, also leads back to 1st century Palestine, again like the Shroud. Cf. Lorenzo

Fig. 104. *Veronica with the Veil*, MS 133 F 9, Dutch Prayer Book, 1480-1500, f. 18v; The Hague, Koninklijke Bibliotheek.

Bianchi, *The Sudarium of Oviedo*, in "30Giorni", 4, 2009.

[160] We find reference to a portrait on canvas visible from both sides written in the life of Raphael by Vasari: "Albrecht Dürer, a most marvellous German painter, and an engraver of very beautiful copperplates, rendered tribute to Raffaello out of his own works, and sent to him a portrait of himself, a head, executed by him in gouache on a cloth of fine linen, which showed the same on either side, the lights being transparent and obtained without lead-white, while the only grounding and colouring was done with water-colours, the white of the cloth serving for the ground of the bright parts. This work seemed to Raffaello to be marvellous, and he sent him, therefore, many drawings executed by his own hand, which were received very gladly by Albrecht." Vasari, *Raffaello da Urbino*.

[161] The hypothesis has not been confirmed yet. Cf. Jan S. Jaworski, *Properties of byssal threads, the chemical nature of their colors and the Veil of Manoppello*, in Proceedings of the International Workshop on the Scientific approach to the Acheiropoietos Images, Frascati, 4-6 maggio 2010.

[162] Nicephorus Callistus Xanthopulus, *Historia Ecclesiastica*, book I, chapter 40. Greek Patrology 145, 748-749. Here Nicephorus takes from the ancestors' texts the somatic features of Jesus and of the Mother and he re-elaborates them in an original manner by adding a few features that complete the portrait.

[163] Museo Nazionale di Palazzo Venezia, Rome.

[164] Pfeiffer, *Il Volto Santo di Manoppello*, op. cit., p. 18.

[165] Donato Vittore, contribution to the conference *Il Volto Santo di Manoppello e l'iconografia dell'immagine di Cristo*, Chieti, Università G. d'Annunzio, February 2006.

[166] Giulio Fanti, *Ricerche scientifiche su immagini acheropite*, at the conference *Il Volto Santo di Manoppello*, Padua, March 20, 2007.

[167] "The different representation of the hair lock on the two Faces (obtained from both sides of the Veil) is interesting because up to now it has not been reproduced in a similar fabric and therefore it is one of the particularities that speak in favor of the hypothesis of an image not made by human hands. It is still unexplained how an artist could have painted a sign on one side of this very fine Veil and a different sign on the reverse side without impressing the same sign on both sides (the capillarity of the byssus yarns must not be neglected)". Jan S. Jaworski, Giulio Fanti, *3-D processing to evidence characteristics represented in Manoppello veil*, in Proceedings of the International Workshop, op. cit. See also Bianchi, *Il velo di Manoppello*, op. cit.

[168] [...] I found in it, with considerable, tender sorrow, the head, pricked by thorns, the forehead covered with blood, the eyes bloodshot and bruised, the face pale, on the right cheek a cruel imprint of the iron gloved hand of Malchus, and on the left, signs of the spitting by the Jews, the nose crushed and bloody, the mouth open, spotted with blood, the teeth displaced, the beard and hair torn in some places, and all of the most Holy Face as bruised as it is full of Majesty, compassion, love and sadness [...]" (Our translation) Carlo Bartolomeo Piazza, *Emerologio di Roma Cristiana, Ecclesiastica e Gentile*, Tomo I, Roma 1713, pp. 110-111.

[169] Hans Memling, *Man of Sorrows*, oil on oak panel, Genoa, Palazzo Bianco.

[170] Paul Badde, *The Face of God*, San Francisco, op. cit., pp. 126 ff.

[171] Antonio Bini, in "Il Volto Santo di Manoppello", 1, 2007, pp. 12-13.

[172] Olivier Clément, *Via Crucis*, published on 10th April 1998 www.vatican.va/holy_father/john_paul_ii/speeches/1998/april/index_it.htm

[173] Bridget of Sweden, *The Revelations of St Bir-

gitta *of Sweden*, New York-Oxford, Oxford University Press, 2006. Bk 4. C. 81.

[174] Nicola Gori, *Un canto d'amore al Volto Santo, biografia della Beata Maria Pierina De Micheli*, Città del Vaticano, Libreria Editrice Vaticana, 2012, p. 29.

[175] John Paul II, *We wish to see Jesus*, Message on the occasion of the XIX World Youth Day, 22 February 2004.

[176] During a conference organized by the national German television station ZDF, broadcast on April 21, 2007. [www.zenit.org/it/articles/il-volto-santo-di-manoppello-e-la-plausibilita-teologica-delle-immagini-acheropite].

[177] http://www.raffackfav.wordpress.com and http://www.bookhours.wordpress.com

[178] Karl Pearson, *Die Fronica*, op. cit., p. 94. Our translation.